ENDURING
AMERICA

by Douglas H. Chadwick

Prepared by the Book Division
National Geographic Society, Washington, D.C.

SEA STACKS MARK THE COASTAL WILDERNESS OF OLYMPIC NATIONAL PARK.

Enduring America

Published by The National Geographic Society

Gilbert M. Grosvenor,
President and Chairman of the Board
Michela A. English,
Senior Vice President

Prepared by The Book Division

William R. Gray, *Vice President and Director*
Charles Kogod, *Assistant Director*
Barbara A. Payne, *Editorial Director*

Staff for this book

Charles Kogod,
Project Editor and Illustrations Editor
Margaret Sedeen, *Text Editor*
Cinda Rose, *Art Director*
Victoria Garrett Jones, Kimberly A. Kostyal,
Rebecca Lescaze, Anne E. Withers,
Researchers
Carl Mehler, *Map Editor*
Lewis R. Bassford,
Production Project Manager
Timothy H. Ewing, Richard S. Wain,
Production
Meredith C. Wilcox, *Illustrations Assistant*
Sandra F. Lotterman, *Editorial Assistant*
Karen F. Edwards, Elizabeth G. Jevons,
Peggy J. Oxford, *Staff Assistants*

Manufacturing and Quality Management

George V. White, *Director*
John T. Dunn, *Associate Director*
Vincent P. Ryan, *Manager*
R. Gary Colbert, *Executive Assistant*

Bryan K. Knedler, *Indexer*

Library of Congress CIP Data: page 199

PAGES 2-3: A MARYLAND WILDLIFE REFUGE
SHELTERS A GREAT BLUE HERON.

WITH ITS HAUNTING HOWL, A COYOTE SALUTES A MONTANA WINTER.

Contents

Foreword

It is easy to forget that throughout most of humankind's existence, the concepts of wilderness and wildlife would have held little meaning. There was nothing else out there. Wildness flowed from one end of the earth to the other, like the seas.

I'm not sure what time means, but I know that for people in increasingly crowded societies propelled by fast-changing technologies, it has become something they never seem to have enough of. However, scattered across the North American continent are realms in which time is still defined mainly by the rhythms of nature, where the turning of a season is a momentous event, and where the passing of centuries has left scarcely a mark.

When the first Paleo-Indian bands arrived from Eurasia across the Bering Land Bridge, toward the close of the Ice Age, they wouldn't have known that they had entered a different continent. They had merely moved across into another part of Beringia, the glacier-free region that included portions of eastern Siberia and Alaska and served as a northerly refuge for life during periods of glacial advance.

Exactly when they embarked on the southward journey that would ultimately take them to the subtropics of Florida and Mexico and beyond is still their secret. But, for a while, this new territory they were discovering held woolly mammoths and giant ground sloths, moose and musk oxen, huge short-faced bears alongside grizzlies, and scimitar-toothed cats together with wolves. The days and nights must have roared with tales of the hunt.

Virtually all the native species found on the continent today were already in existence as the Pleistocene gave way to the modern climatic epoch we call the Holocene. The Indians went on to flourish among them. For the most part their cultures were woven directly into the fabric of nature. They did not perceive bears, eagles, mice, or turtles moving through the forests and meadows. They saw Bear People, Eagle People, Mouse People, and Turtle People, all with languages, societies, and special powers of their own. And they saw themselves as brothers, sisters, daughters, sons—clansmen and clanswomen of those creatures with whom they shared the land and waters. The Indians hunted them, just as the animals hunted other animals to live. Yet the Indians also learned from the animals, as students from teachers, talked to them, prayed to them, received dreams from them, imitated them in sacred dances, and, in their visions, sometimes changed shape with them.

Then came another wave of colonization, beginning at the continent's opposite shore. The new immigrants were Europeans. According to their moral view, a fundamental and unbridgeable gulf separated humans from all other forms of life. They saw their destiny in terms of subjugating the wilderness, saving souls, and accumulating wealth. In the process of imposing their culture upon the New World, these white people would transform most of the ecosystems they encountered almost beyond recognition.

I have spent years hiking through some of the last great stretches of backcountry that remain, trying to get far enough and deep enough in to glimpse what the world might have been like when time was measured chiefly by flowerings, migrations, and the wheeling of the stars. I go partly just to enjoy the splendors of the wild creatures and terrain, and partly on a very personal quest, seeking to rediscover the ancient, vital connections that exist between one wild creature and another and between their communities, the land, and ourselves. What I'm really after, I suppose, is a certain sense of wholeness and continuity that seems harder and harder to find elsewhere.

Some 10,000 years have passed since the Holocene began. I know I'm getting close to a good place to camp when I can no longer tell for sure which one of those years the day around me belongs to. For perspective I often imagine that it is 1491, the year before the ships of Christopher Columbus first anchored off the coast of the New World. I invite you to leave your watch and calendar at home and come with me in search of the enduring natural power and bounty of this continent that would come to be called North America.

Douglas H. Chadwick

A RAVEN TOTEM WATCHES OVER THE WORLD OF RAVEN'S CREATURES.

Land of Wolf and Raven

Listen to the voice. It is strong and sure, greedy and lusty and questioning and mysterious all at once, full of power. Full of life. Cr-r-ruck! And you will hear it everywhere, from the highest mountains to the beaches, for Raven lives wherever he pleases. In the beginning, before there was time, he made the sun and moon and stars. This is why sacred rattles used by shamans show him with the sun or moon in his mouth. Raven made the earth, too, and all the living things so that there would be crowberries and whale blubber and caribou meat and wolves to sing in the night. Some say Raven also made people. Others say people formed inside a huge clam and Raven only pried the shell open to let them out. The way Bering Strait Eskimo people tell the story, Raven was walking by the sea when he came upon the first human. He asked the man how he came to be and discovered that the human had been growing inside the pod of a beach pea for four days. On the fifth day

An arctic fox pauses amid a vast landscape that evokes the Arctic

world known by the first Americans as they crossed Beringia from Asia.

the human finally uncoiled, split the green capsule, and burst forth. When he learned this, Raven said, "I made the beach and the vine the pods grow from. But I never imagined that something like you would come out of it."

Spring has finally reached all the way north to touch the Arctic. Each dawn now promises more open ground than the last. Across the tundra, meltwater is gathering at the base of sedge hummocks, seeping through dwarf willow stems, trickling toward the wide, gravel-strewn floodplain, slowly swelling the braided river channels. Winter has not yet retreated all that far, though. It slips back to harden the ground at night, and the morning wind blowing down off the peaks feels sharp as the edge of frost-split stone.

In a broad valley roughed out between a jumble of foothills, two animals cross the river on a bridge of leftover ice and pick their way up a slope among scattered boulders. Nearing the base of a cliff, they come upon a Dall sheep that proved unable to outlast the final cold snap of the season. Partially sunken into a cushion of lichen and newly green moss, its weathered horn spirals up to point at the highest summit within view, as if by way of final tribute. The pair pause to inspect the remains, touching them hesitantly. Then they lie down close to a boulder to rest out of the wind for a few moments and absorb what they can of the sun's faint heat, letting their gaze drift across the folded countryside beyond.

As far as their eyes can see—as far as any eyes can see—there is only more elemental, untamed topography: rock and river and sky and tundra without end and perhaps, somewhere, a few more of their kind. But what kind are they, this pair of animals? They are wolves. They are caribou. They are more snow-white Dall sheep. Shaggy musk oxen. Great, silver-tipped bears. Blue-phase arctic foxes with coats the color of ice deep in crevasses. They are early Americans robed in fur and carrying spears. They are modern Americans packing nylon tents and freeze-dried food. In many ways, it doesn't matter. Not here in Alaska's Brooks Range. Here, what counts is how much they have in common.

The Arctic and subarctic latitudes encompass nearly all of Alaska and the greater part of Canada, from the Yukon across to Labrador and Newfoundland. This is the land of tundra and taiga. Largest of the continent's major biogeographic regions, it is the harshest in terms of climate and the least altered by human development. Immense tracts of primal America can be found throughout the region, set aside as reserves, linking the past to the future. These huge, interconnected sanctuaries conserve far more than a sampling of native wildlife and scenery. They safeguard the possibility of really understanding what the world was like when nature was bounded only by more nature.

So long silent except for the sighing of the wind and the hiss of dry, driven snow, the country around the pair of animals is filling with voices. Both rock ptarmigan and willow ptarmigan males are everywhere, advertising themselves to hens with loud croaks and cacklings. Although their feet are still webbed with the feathers that helped insulate their legs while serving as snowshoes during the winter, their whole plumage is changing, like the tundra, from white to mottled brown.

For two-thirds of the year, the arctic ground squirrels lay underground in suspended animation like bulbs of wild onions or spring beauties. Now, revived, they are eating the first shoots of those plants and conversing in chirps and whistles. Like many northern mammals, they tend to be larger than their counterparts to the south, greater bulk being an advantage in withstanding cold. Not surprisingly, they are also more thickly furred. The people here—Inuit, Inupiat, and the widespread Athapaskan, or Dene, tribes—call these tunnelers parka squirrels and traditionally quilted the hides into warm coats for themselves.

Following an especially loud, high chirp, the land abruptly goes quiet again. The ptarmigan crouch among the low-growing crowberry and lapland rosebay, heads cocked so that one eye gazes straight up. The pair of travelers are looking skyward too, for they have learned that while ground squirrels chatter shrilly to warn of a predator afoot, a single alarm whistle means danger from the air. And there, overhead, appears the hunter, stroking through the air currents on wings like scythe blades.

A number of peregrine falcons nest in cliffs and banks in this land beyond the tree

Arctic and Subarctic

line. No avalanche off the peaks, no snowflake hurtling before blizzard winds, nor any living creature moves faster than a peregrine diving toward a target; it can reach more than 200 miles an hour. But the bird above the travelers is a gyrfalcon, the largest falcon in the world, and it hunts by flying hard and low, hugging the contours of the terrain.

Failing to flush any prey from cover, the falcon banks steeply upward to circle the area and finally wings away over the nearest ridge. As it does, the ptarmigan gradually resume their calling. Ground squirrel noses emerge from the shadowy holes, and the pair of animals rise to resume their journey. It is as if spring itself, having paused for the briefest of moments, were stretching again and preparing to move on.

The awakening quickens. One day, the plain sloping from the mountains to the frozen sea is an empty expanse of tundra mixed with shrinking snowfields and slushy pools, shrouded by chill fog blowing in off the ice pack. The following day brings cries from the ravens, one of the few birds besides the ptarmigan hardy enough to live here year-round. Different from the birds' usual raucous yells, the sounds are a mixture of low "quorks"; hollow-sounding knocks, as if someone were drumming on driftwood; and a singular, riveting noise like that of a struck gong. As with much of the raven's varied vocabulary, the meaning of such calls is mysterious, but they tend to arise when the birds encounter something intriguing. They carry news through the mist.

That afternoon, the air clears to reveal a sprinkling of caribou that have crossed the mountains from the south. The sprinkling seems to thicken with each passing hour until the fog rolls in again. Two weeks later, it is as if the North Slope had sprouted a forest, for caribou groups stand scattered above the tundra by the tens of thousands.

This is natural magic, the conjuring of life upon barren-looking ground. And it has only just begun. Tawny calves, still wet from the fluids that have bathed them in the womb, soon materialize between the legs of the adults. Within a few hours, the babies are able to keep up with their mothers at a walk. The young ones themselves don't actually walk so much as follow along in outbursts of wobbly skittering. Still, every step, every pronk and splayed-leg landing, builds vital coordination. Before they are three days old, they will be able to outrun a human and, some four weeks after that, a wolf, bear, or wolverine. Caribou calves are exactly as strong and precocious as generations of northern predators have combined to make them.

Land of Wolf and Raven

Through the rest of May and June the calves nurse while the mothers graze sprouting sedges and shrubs. The seabirds called jaegers, themselves rearing young on the coastal flats, go kiting by overhead, seeking lemmings and voles forced from cover by the hoofs plunging down beside them. Around the first week of July the caribou begin to group into bands. Then herds, then still more massive congregations. Ultimately, they become a single, 100,000-headed organism that surges across the countryside like a geologic force, blanketing foothills, gouging out pathways, practically damming rivers during crossings. Then, even more suddenly than they arrived, they are gone, bearing toward winter ranges far to the south. They leave the tundra cropped down, scored with trails, and enriched by dung—and yet somehow more empty-feeling than it was to start with, as if the whole spectacle had been dreamed.

In a time that could be a thousand summers and migrations ago, a rivulet of caribou sweeps down off a pass into a valley. All at once, those in the forefront look up to find a line of wolves striding parallel to them farther up the hillside. The pack is led by a four-year-old, gray animal with a black neck ruff and an intent golden stare. She is the alpha female, who produced a litter of five this year. Recently weaned, the pups are back at the pack's rendezvous site in the company of an aunt. This is the first time the alpha female has gone off hunting with the other adults since her babies were born.

The caribou nervously raise their tails. Mothers nuzzle their calves, reassuring themselves that the young ones are close. A few stamp the broad, splayed hoofs that distribute their weight on snow and spongy ground. Typically, though, they make no move to flee. They seem to possess an inborn confidence in their ability to outrun enemies. Besides, a predator that detects no obviously weak or straggling animals may decide to turn aside. The caribou will not bolt until they have verified the threat by scent. The wolves know this, and the caribou know it. It is a mutual sizing up—a game as old as their kind.

17

Almost imperceptibly, the she-wolf turns downhill at an angle that will intercept the herd. Just as subtly, the herd adjusts its course away. The dance continues until, in an eye blink, the wolf accelerates from a fast walk to a run. The valley explodes with the sound of hoofbeats. Though racing full-out now, the wolves draw no closer to the nearest prey. Ahead, where the river bends, rock ledges project from the hillsides, constricting the valley. When the caribou start to swing through that turn, two wolves that have taken a shortcut higher on the slope dash from behind the outcrop, blocking the flight of several animals.

In the confusion, one inexperienced calf panics and begins to turn back rather than racing at its mother's heels. It is met by the wolves coming from behind. The alpha female grabs its nose. The mother caribou rushes at the attackers. Dodging her, a fourth wolf takes the outstretched calf by the neck. A fifth bites into the soft groin. The mother wheels and gallops off after the herd. Within minutes, the pack is feeding, growling, and vying for position where the calf has been opened up.

*H*ours later, more hunters wend their way through the valley. Each is carrying a quarter of a grown caribou over his shoulder and taking a turn in the singing of a traveling tale. The men wear tough caribou-hide boots on their feet and amulets of carved stone. Most of the other things they possess, from summer shirts to the sinews wrapping spear points to hafts of alder, come from caribou. They are aware that even the flesh of their bodies comes largely from the caribou. Except for the brief time that the caribou are on their remote calving grounds, the men have stalked little else.

Before this last hunt, they spoke to the caribou once again, asking the animals to let themselves be killed and promising to honor their spirits. And they felt sure the caribou were listening, for everything went well. Like the wolves, some of the men hurried ahead to await the herd at a defile. Rows of stone cairns built there by earlier hunters would help funnel the quarry up against a cliff face. The men were in place and ready when the herd came stampeding toward them, driven by the other members of the hunting party. Seven animals were taken, more than the men could carry. They dug pits into the permafrost to cache the extra meat until they could return.

Now, bound homeward to the campsite where their families wait, the men see ravens scattering before them and know that some other hunter has had luck with the caribou. In case it is Bear, they approach with caution, only to find wolves walking grudgingly away from the carcass. The men notice older, bleached bones strewn about and understand that this is not the first time the wolves have made an ambush here.

The lead man remembers a year when the caribou failed to come on any of the expected routes. His people went into winter with a pitifully small store of dried meat. It was a year of mothers who had no milk for their babies and of elders crushing willow bark into medicines. And of wailing for the dead. Raising his hand in salute to the pack now regrouped on a ledge some distance above, he calls out: *Ho, Wolf With Eyes Like the Sun. Ho, Wolf Who Walks Hurt. It has been a good day for hunting. A time of plenty for all.*

The wolves remain silent, swiveling their ears. Only a raven answers with three quick, brazen croaks, tilting its head to fix the passersby with a piercing look, as if to say, "Ah, never when I made the world did I imagine that something like you would come out of it." The men march on, resuming their song. They are nearly two miles downstream before they hear a familiar chorus of notes echoing through the valley. Pausing to shift their loads, they nod at one another. The wolves are singing too.

The permafrost layer underlying most tundra and taiga begins close to the surface. Soils that develop above it are generally thin, boggy, and acidic. They support a limited range of plants. Many of those contain chemical compounds in their leaves that make them unpalatable or, at most, poor-quality forage. Many are slow-growing, given the brief summers at such latitudes. So although this region is home to a majestic array of large animals, there isn't food to support many of them in any one area for long. This is why the caribou migrate along circuits covering hundreds or even thousands of miles in a year. And why, although the territory of a wolf pack takes in 50 to 200 square miles in the Great Lakes region, it easily covers ten times that much ground in the Arctic.

There is another major food chain here, though, and it begins in freshwater. With the uppermost layers of ground melting and the snowpack melting, lowland tundra becomes, in effect, one vast, sodden bog interlaced with an almost infinite number of shallow pools. No sooner does the thaw get underway than birds of all sizes start to show up from distant wintering grounds as if drawn along the magnetic lines converging toward the Pole. Tundra swans, geese, ducks, and sandhill cranes flock in from the southern part of the continent; sandpipers from its plains and coasts; phalaropes from the open ocean; golden plovers and wandering tattlers from South America and the Pacific; wheatears, bluethroats, and yellow wagtails from Asia and Africa; and arctic terns from their wintering grounds near the South Pole 10,000 miles away.

The sooner a bird arrives, the better its chances of claiming a good territory. Beyond that, many larger species have no choice but to begin nesting as early as possible. They are in a race to rear their slow-developing young to flight stage before the country freezes up again in fall. The reasons they have come so far north to begin with can be found wriggling and pulsing all around them: insects. Midges, craneflies, and, mosquitoes, most of which begin as aquatic larvae.

Many caribou on the North Slope benefit from the cool air off the ice pack that causes the insect hordes to emerge later than elsewhere and keeps them down on many days once they are out. In other areas caribou go fairly high up in the mountains, seeking out the cold, gusty, bug-damping conditions. During a spell of warm, windless weather these northernmost members of the deer family are so busy shaking their heads and stamping their feet while grazing that you wonder if they aren't burning up more calories than they are taking in. When the time comes to rest, they seek out lingering snowfields and bed down close to the center, where fewer insects can reach them. The wolves and foxes lie curled with noses buried in their bushy tails, much as they would during a winter blizzard, while the mosquitoes close around them in a humming, gray mist—tiny predators in a very large pack.

Yet, for the birds, the profusion of six-legged life is concentrated protein to be pulled from the mud with long, probing beaks, plucked from plant stems, strained through flattened bills, or snatched on the wing. Phalaropes pirouette in shallow ponds until they create little whirlpools that suck up bottom debris swirling with larvae. Mergansers and goldeneye ducks hunt the fish that have been fattening on the bugs. Although other waterfowl may prefer plant food, their young rely heavily upon emerging adult insects during their first weeks of life.

Land of Wolf and Raven

Out where the pack ice growls and polar bears roam between seal breathing holes, a different aquatic food chain is about to appear. As the floes loosen at their seam with the shore and gradually retreat through the summer, microscopic life blooms among the blue waves. Bowhead whales, each plankton-scooping head larger than the rest of the body, spew great plumes of moist breath as they surface. Seabirds and kayaks ply the path alongside them. Char run upstream toward spawning beds, passing resident grayling, which seem to have northern lights shimmering in their sail-like dorsal fins.

Along the riverbanks, grizzlies dig in the gravel bars for starchy roots of the purple-flowered legume known as bear root, or Eskimo potato. Musk oxen snip louseworts, whose stalks produce clusters of blossoms shaped like woolly, trunked heads of mammoths. Flowering dryads, heathers, ground-hugging azaleas, and arctic poppies flare from the shores up the hillsides. Through the late hours, the midnight sun tints the mountain walls and the glaciers themselves the hues of petals, loon eyes, and the rosy, glittering scales on the bellies of the char.

Several days' journey to the south, in the taiga, an old hunter announces to his family: "I will go to the clearing by the lake where the big pike live. A moose is coming there early in the afternoon. I have seen him in my mind." When he returns in the evening to ask for help carrying the meat he has killed, no one is surprised. Does this imply that people do have visions that foretell the future? Or simply that when all that surrounds you and sustains you over a lifetime derives directly from wildness, you become so attuned to subtle clues and patterns that you can predict what an animal will do? Is there a real difference between the first possibility and the second? Living systems are networks of miracles large and small. There are many ways of understanding them and many strands yet to be revealed.

The remains of the hunter's moose lie next to a white spruce. Together with black spruce, which favors more sodden ground, this conifer dominates the taiga—the land of little trees. It seems that some of the white spruce always have clumps of stunted branches near or below the crown. The cause is a common rust fungus that stimulates the twigs to grow into dense, ball-like forms. Northern red and flying squirrels use the clumps as nests, resting spots, and places to cache dry mushrooms. One of the chief mushrooms in the squirrels' diet happens to be quite different—truffles and truffle-like fungi that grow underground. As the squirrels race back and forth between branch clumps, their droppings seed the forest floor with spores from the fungi they have been eating.

Most plant roots are associated with massed fungal threads called mycorrhizae. In return for traces of sugar and starch produced by the plant, the mycorrhizae take up moisture and nutrients from tiny crevices between the soil particles. This symbiotic relationship can be especially crucial to plants struggling to survive under marginal conditions. Living at the northern edge of the tree line where soil temperatures are low and nutrients scarce, white spruce rely upon several types of mycorrhizae. They are those whose fruiting bodies are gathered by the squirrels.

The rust fungus that produces the clumped spruce branches requires an alternate host, which turns out to be subarctic bearberry and Labrador tea. Changes in the condition of these plants affect berry pickers from white-crowned sparrows and ptarmigan to foxes and grizzlies. The squirrels themselves eat the berries. So do weasels and the squirrels' main predator, the pine marten, and, of course, people. In short, what appears at first as an isolated and obscure case of spruce blight turns out to be an intersection of processes animating the taiga.

With the onset of fall, caribou from the North Slope are dispersing in scattered bands toward the taiga. Insects are swarming out across the world in the form of a million new feathered wings. Some of the migratory birds will have stayed behind, transmuted into ravens, which raided eggs and nestlings; into foxes, whose parents returned to the den bearing mouthfuls of chicks; into gyrfalcons, which struck like arrows; and even into grizzly bears, which preyed upon nesting geese in some areas.

For a brief, dazzling time, the landscape is flushed gold and burgundy. Then, inevitably, comes the reign of winter. For the next eight months, the surface of the earth will stay crystallized. And of all the life that has touched upon it, there will sometimes be only a single black raven against a landscape of unbroken white and, farther toward the horizon, the tracks of a wolf fast disappearing beneath the drifting snow.

COTTONWOOD AND SPRUCE TREES HAVE GROWN IN THE ARCTIC FOR 10,000 YEARS.

*N*omads of the Arctic infinity, caribou follow the seasons,
migrating hundreds of miles between winter ranges and spring calving
grounds (opposite, left). Forage includes sedges, grasses, forbs, willow
and birch leaves, and lichens. The animals often travel in herds so
large that they seem to have neither beginning nor end.

*P*olar bears range the northland, their footprints sometimes shadowed by the small prints (right) of a scavenging arctic fox. Bear habitat skirts frigid seas, where the animals stalk seals or walrus from pack ice or floes. But life is not all work. It also brings playful roughhousing with a mate or a snooze in the snow.

Preceding pages: The Kuskokwim River sprawls across Alaska to the sea.

Twin cubs, hitching a ride with their mother, will hone their instinctive

swimming agility. During their second winter they will learn to hunt seals.

*R*enewal and endurance mark the cycle of northern seasons. Only hours old, a trumpeter swan cygnet nestles amid lily pads. At summer's end it will fly south with its parents. When winter descends, the raven prevails, ever wise, sly, playful, hardy— a mythic creature sacred to Arctic peoples.

*E*nergy blazes in the dash of a quick red fox and in
the charged particles from the sun that shimmer in the aurora
borealis. Eskimo legend saw, in the aurora, images of deceased
family and friends dancing around the heavenly fires.

Shrouded by fog, a bull moose in rut cautiously approaches a possible

mate. Cows sometimes pursue a male, grunting and mooing.

*S*pring breakup comes to the Bering Sea, creating a tapestry
of ice floes, many of which serve as walrus calving grounds. These
bulls, taking their summer ease on an island sanctuary, will join
cows and calves out on the ice later in the summer.

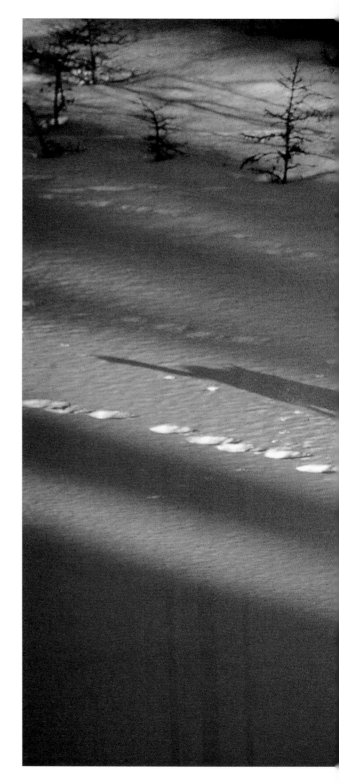

*F*rom its golden eyes to its moonlit sprint, the gray wolf represents wildness and a long-gone time when the wolf was a vital link in nature's chain of being.

Following pages: An arctic wolf leaps floes in northern Canada.

KILLER WHALES AND HUMAN FACES WERE ETCHED AGES AGO ON ROCKS ALONG THE NORTHWEST COAST.

Land of Salmon and Bear

Salmon is coming / Salmon is coming home from the sea / From the sea he is leaping / Dancing in the white waters / He is coming to feed all the people / Salmon, my fish trap is beautiful / I am waiting for you / Here on the bank of Five Rapids River / I sing the songs you taught us / In the days when all beings lived in one lodge.

Salmon is coming. The fish are gathering in the bay, turning it silver and coppery red with their numbers. Their bodies all point one direction toward the river's mouth, the tails slowly waving back and forth like kelp fronds in a tidal current. Every so often, several hundred begin to lash the water at almost the same time, and a wave of fish surges into the river's entrance and up the channel of the fresh waters in which they were born. This is the summer run of chinook, or king, salmon, largest of the seven salmon species spawned in watersheds along the continent's

*I*n Katmai National Park, near where Eskimos lived hundreds of

years ago, Alaskan brown bears and gulls gather to feed on salmon.

Pacific coast. After hatching, they spent at least part of a year in the stream of their birth. They then moved out to the coastal waters and finally to the open ocean, wheeling northward through the Gulf of Alaska. Now, after two to four years at sea, they have returned to lay eggs and begin the cycle anew.

With their rich, pink flesh and prodigious numbers, salmon were a mainstay both of coastal Indian cultures and of many tribes upstream along the great riverways of the West. The fish still play vital roles in native economies and ceremonial life. They come as they have since the mountains rose and the rivers began flowing, leaping up cascades, thrashing their way through the shallows with their backs half out of the water, fighting over nesting territories, and scooping out spawning pits, called redds, in the gravel with their tails. When the swimmers are chinook, it is perhaps easier to understand the old legends of Salmon People, for the biggest among these fish are more than five feet long and weigh up to 125 pounds. They are the size of humans.

The two-legged people wait with their nets and fish traps, and some sing the songs passed on by grandparents, who waited on the same shores. Salmon is coming, rippling, diving, heavy with eggs, from the sea to the people. But the first to catch Salmon are not the people but Bear.

The animal moves in his heavy, swinging bear walk, following the meanders of a nameless creek through a meadow near the coast. Around him is a forest of cedar and hemlock—ancient ones. Elders of their tribe. Some, with trunks thick as four bears, have seen a thousand summers of chinook passing upstream. He was feeding beneath their branches all morning, tearing apart rotted logs to get at the fat grubs inside.

Although the forest floor lay deep in shadow, the meadow is broad and grassy and full of sun where the creek runs through it. The riffles are full of big fish splashing and circling their redds, part of the play of music and reflected light among the waters. A water ouzel, or dipper, flies past, low over the stream course. Landing on an exposed rock, it gives out a bright spray of notes, then wades into the main current and disappears underwater. Thirty seconds later, as if immune to the force of the flow, the plump, gray bird emerges from the same spot with a beak full of caddisfly larvae and mayfly nymphs.

As the bear passes upstream, a harlequin duck hen, followed by four young half her size, breaks from the shore's edge into open water. The mother is molting her worn feathers. She can no more take to the air than her still flightless brood can, and this is a wary time for them. Once out in the current, though, the ducks relax their guard and soon turn to diving for food in a pool eddying behind a boulder. Suddenly, the hen pops up from the water with wings beating frantically and patters across the surface as if a monster were chasing her. One is. Rather than probing among the bottom stones for her usual insect fare, she was pilfering salmon caviar and drew the attention of the female chinook guarding the redd. The fish erupts open-mouthed from the water right after the duck, narrowly missing her tailfeathers.

The flurry catches the bear's attention. He pauses, and his gaze settles on a fish hovering over a shallow strand of pebbles. He lunges off the bank toward it. Swats with one great paw. Misses. The creek boils with sleek bodies torpedoing off in every direction. Excited, he splashes upstream after them, veering from one toward the next.

The bear stops after a while and shakes himself. He has not had much luck with this technique of chasing through the stream. Most of the fish are just in from the sea and still too strong and fast to pin with a paw. With each passing day, however, the advantage will shift his way, for salmon undergo a fundamental change in metabolism as soon as they enter freshwater. All but the steelhead cease eating for good and begin living off stored reserves, and their tissues begin to deteriorate. After spawning, they have but one destiny, and that is to perish. Yet the nutrients they have gathered from the ocean and carried upstream will enrich both the channel in which their fry develop and the entire ecosystem around it.

Farther on, the bear reaches the deep, green pool at the base of a cascade where salmon gather between attempts to hurdle the steep, white water. The pool's center already holds one bear. Standing submerged to its neck, it is catching salmon by clutching them against its chest. A second bear swims nearby with its head underwater like a burly

Far West

49

otter. Barely a paw's swipe away, a red fox tugs the remaining meat from a cast-off fish carcass. And just out of reach of the fox, gulls and ravens scavenge spilled roe and older remains. From the branches of an overhanging snag, two bald eagles survey the scene, waiting for larger scraps to appear.

Approaching cautiously through the brush, the male finds another bear leaning out over the bank to swipe at passing fish with one paw. He also finds two cubs wrestling at her side. The mother turns to face him, flattening her ears. She begins to whuff and then make a popping sound by snapping her jaws together—a direct threat. The male backs away to look for another fishing site. The one he settles for is far from the best. But the base of the cascade is so choked with fish that a few of those exhausted by failed leaps drift down his way from time to time. He eventually manages to grab one with a quick bite. He drags the flapping salmon to shore and plonks down on his haunches to begin devouring it while the birds gather noisily beside him to await their turn.

At last, Bear has his fish, the first of many to come. Each will count heavily in the contest to put on enough fat to outlast six months of winter in his den. The more he can add, the better his condition will be when he emerges and the better his chances of claiming a mate and breeding as spring turns into another salmon summer.

*T*he land of Salmon and Bear and their fellow creatures extends from Alaska's Panhandle southward to northern Baja California and from the Pacific Northwest east to the Continental Divide. It is, for the most part, a realm of deep evergreen forests and towering mountains, all veined with powerful rivers.

Not that long ago, this was also the land of Raven and Wolf, for as in much of the Arctic and subarctic, Wolf ranged throughout, from the seas to the peaks, while Raven played a central role in Indian mythology. It was Raven who created the waters and the salmon, which came to sacrifice themselves to the people; Raven who fashioned every creature that walks or flies; Raven who helped the worthy but loved to trick the unsuspecting; Raven, as full of mischief as he was wonderful, who made this world the way it is.

In Indian times, a bear fishing for salmon anywhere along the seaboard could have been a brown bear: *Ursus arctos horribilis*, whose silver-tipped form is better known as the grizzly. Only black bears fish the coastal streams south of British Columbia now; Great Bear—Real Bear, Bear That Walks Like a Man—is gone from the Pacific states. So are nearly 90 percent of the old-growth forests. The remainder lie mostly scattered in fragments. But in Washington's Olympic Peninsula, where nearly 923,000 primeval acres have been set aside as Olympic National Park, you can yet find a path that leads into the sword ferns beneath the giant trees and beyond the reach of time.

The westernmost section of the park is a strip that includes the outer coast with its long strands of gravel beach interspersed with stream deltas and headlands. Just offshore jut the craggy islets called sea stacks. They were the headlands millions of waves ago. Now and then, a storm erodes another section of the main shoreline to reveal long-buried remains of the Makah or Quileute cultures. The most common are middens, or refuse heaps, full of ordinary clam shells and the bones of salmon and herring. But sometimes the earth slumps away to expose artifacts such as pieces of paddles from seagoing canoes and harpoon tips that speak of the tribes' lives as hunters of northern fur seals and the gray whales that migrate up and down the coast each year from Baja California to the Gulf of Alaska.

The Pacific coast Indians lived between two of the biologically richest forests in North America. One lies mostly hidden underwater, out where the heads of seals and California sea lions show among the swells. With species whose stalks grow to a length of a hundred feet, a Pacific Northwest kelp forest may produce as much biomass per acre as an equatorial rain forest. These marine jungles provide crucial food and shelter for the juveniles of a great many oceangoing fish. Young gray whales will come in and hide among the tangles to escape killer whales. Mink and raccoons probe the tide pools, while river otters sometimes swim out to hunt in the salt water like their close kin, the sea otters.

As the kelp washes ashore, its fronds and the sea creatures stranded within them draw black bears, Columbian black-tailed deer, coyotes, and ravens to the beaches. They come from the second forest—the spired kingdom of western red cedar, western hemlock, Sitka spruce, and Douglas fir. It is the lushest conifer woodland in the world and the continent's only temperate rain forest, watered by as many as 200 inches of rainfall each year. As in the tropics, branches are laden with mats of epiphytic mosses and ferns. They also hold pine martens, pileated woodpeckers, and the nests of marbled murrelets, which fly to and from feeding grounds at sea. Spotted owls perch waiting for nightfall, avoiding more open woodlands. Among their prey are northern flying squirrels and the tree phenacomys, a mouse-size rodent that may live out its entire life without ever leaving the high canopy.

Beneath the trees, Roosevelt elk pick their way among the ground cover, grazing twisted stalk or false Solomon's seal or perhaps the young shoots of salmonberry, which Indian women also gathered for food before the berries appeared. And beneath the elk, a diverse assortment of snails and slugs graze decaying leaf litter and molds. The fungi are everywhere. Some glow like luminous sea creatures. Through their network of threads, others bring food to wildflowers pale as morning fog, such as Indian pipe or phantom orchid, which have no powers of photosynthesis.

A huge conifer toppled onto the forest floor may take three to five centuries to decompose. In this lengthy process of going to pieces, the wooden corpses become spongy reservoirs of water that help keep the local environment fairly damp even during spells of dry weather. They become nutrient storehouses as well, accumulating nitrogen produced by bacterial activity, and these nurse logs serve as the most common site for conifer seedlings to germinate and establish themselves.

In the rain forest's depths, you can scarcely find anything that is not of, by, or from living material. The very stones are cloaked with mosses and organic duff. It is as if you had been taken into the emerald core of some colossal, multifaceted organism. Like salmon, the nurse logs symbolize nature's never ending creation of new strength from old, of splendor from decay. If you walk among them long enough in the mist-thickened, cathedral light that filters down through the canopy, you might even come out a little less afraid of death than before.

Traveling with Salmon up the mightiest of Pacific river systems south of Canada, the Columbia, we would be some 900 miles inland before reaching one of the farthest spawning grounds, in Idaho. The salmon stop earlier elsewhere in part because they simply cannot make it over one more modern dam. Still, the headwaters remain home to native bull trout and cutthroat trout. They continue up the sides of the Rockies until the flow becomes too small or the waterfalls too high. From that point, for hikers, it is not far through the forests of subalpine fir to the high-country tundra and on to the tip-top of the Continental Divide. Having started among mussel beds at sea level, we have come to the realm of thin air and alpenglow, where bearded beasts the color of lingering snow stand sentinel.

The mountain goat looks from the hikers back to the panorama falling away from her feet. Her chief concern is her offspring, working its way across a series of thin ledges toward her. Since late May, when the kid was born, the nanny has spent a large share of each day positioning herself directly below the infant so that if it slipped, it would land against her legs rather than the next ledge down. Given where they live, that ledge might be a couple of feet below or a couple of hundred.

When not nursing or resting on its side, the kid is in constant motion, jumping and tossing its horns and, most of all, trying to scramble up anything with an imposing slope—including its mother when she lies down. But this is only what you might expect in a hoofed creature that within a few short months must be able to traverse cliff faces so icy and precipitous that not even snow can stick to them for long. Here on the sudden edge of stone and sky, high spirits are an essential ingredient for survival—high spirits and a patient, ever vigilant mother.

As she works her way around a promontory, the nanny's attention turns to a golden eagle gliding near on a thermal. She makes a mewling bleat that brings her young one running to take cover between her legs, then stamps a forefoot and tosses her horns in the bird's direction. As her reactions suggest, both bald and golden eagles occasionally snatch newborn goats. They may also try to knock an older animal loose from a precarious foothold so they can feast on the broken body below. But this eagle is scanning a flower-lit meadow below for hoary marmots and

Columbian ground squirrels, and it drifts on by without a glance at the white climbers.

Few predators besides the eagle can get close to mountain goats, and any that do stand a good chance of being gored by the climbers' stiletto-sharp horns. However, in return for the security from carnivores that comes from living higher and steeper than any other large animal in North America, the goats must contend not only with climbing accidents but with avalanches, rockfalls, severe storms, and starvation, particularly of the kids and yearlings, over the cold months.

Like their patchy winter food supply—a few wind-stunted fir trees here, a cluster of Douglas maple shrubs there, several tiers of snow-free, grassy ledges up near the ridgeline—goats stay spread out in relatively small bands. The trait that helps keep groups small and separate is aggression. Whenever goats come very close to one another, quarrels are sooner or later going to break out. Even though most involve no more than tense posturing or a bluff charge, stabbings do happen. Subordinate animals can also get prodded off a ledge to an uncertain fate.

Here is one more reason for nannies to be protective of their kids, which are the lowest-ranking goats in the social hierarchy. It is why the nanny near the divide is now paying so much attention to the approach of a band containing another nanny and kid, two yearlings, and a two-year-old billy. The kids no sooner spy one another than they rush together and start to frolic. By a sort of mutual consent, the mothers stand back to let them try out their bumbling versions of adult courtship and fighting patterns. Yet as soon as the young billy draws near her kid, the first nanny stalks toward him in a stiff, threatening posture.

Rather than yield, this subadult male arches stiffly in turn. However, a kind of loose shake of his head hints that he is not all that serious about the confrontation. He is in it for the excitement. This is the height of summer; everyone is full of wildflower blossoms and succulent herbs, curiosity and spunk. Noticing the two older goats begin to circle head-to-tail, the first kid breaks off playing and charges over to his mother's opponent. There he proceeds to lacerate the air all around one of the billy's knees with horns that barely show as nubbins.

Stimulated in turn, yet apparently reluctant to risk more jousting with the increasingly annoyed nanny, the billy wheels away to go leaping and sliding down a sharply inclined snowbank, tossing his horns and spinning completely around in midair. The kid follows right after him and spins so hard that it falls onto its side in a spray of crystals. And the nanny once again follows after her kid. At first, she merely trots down the hard corn snow. Yet a slip leads to a slide, a slide to a toss of the horns, and before she is halfway to the bottom, she, too, is making spinning leaps.

Such outbursts are fairly common among mountain goats during the warm months—especially when they have an opportunity to glissade down leftover snow. Since the display contains so many elements of aggression, you could call it a war dance. Or you could just recognize that even grown-up animals in one of the most physically demanding of all niches have their share of fun.

 substantial portion of the wildest lands left in the contiguous 48 states lies high in the heart of the Rockies. It includes three especially grand tracts, beginning with the one focused around 2.2-million-acre Yellowstone National Park. The second runs from east-central Idaho into western Montana and consists of the adjoining Selway Bitterroot and Frank Church-River of No Return wilderness areas. The third is made up of Montana's Scapegoat, Bob Marshall, and Great Bear wilderness areas plus Glacier National Park. Mountain ranges and other largely undeveloped country form corridors most of the way between the three tracts, and Glacier is linked in turn to Waterton National Park in Alberta and other Canadian wildlands still farther north. Biologists refer to this array as the central Rocky Mountain ecosystem, and in its large, interconnected landscapes they see one of the best hopes anywhere in the contiguous states for big, wide-ranging animals to carry on their natural patterns of survival and evolution.

Glacier hosts almost every species present in the Rockies since the end of the Ice Age. But then the Ice Age doesn't seem to have ended all that long ago here. Dozens of small but active glaciers linger in the high country among peaks that still look freshly hewn. Mountain goats, the official symbol of the park, share the lower cliff faces and scree slopes with bighorn sheep. Moose browse the bottomlands together with elk, mule deer and white-tailed deer. Mountain lions stalk the coniferous forest along with lynx. Coyote tracks intersect those of wolves, which recently recolonized to Montana from Canada, and the woodlands hold both grizzlies and black bears.

In a community this vital and complex, a change in the grizzly population, for example, leads to shifts in black bear home ranges and then to differences in survival and reproduction among the wolves, cougars, and coyotes, which compete with the bears either for live food, carcasses to scavenge, or both. The natural balance, therefore, is not just between predator and prey. It is also between one type of big carnivore and another, and between one race of hoofed animal and another, each with its own balance of strengths, skills, and learning abilities. The permutations are fascinating and virtually infinite, and modern science has a very long way to go to understand how they work. What we have begun to see is that, in the long run, they add to the ecosystem's overall stability. And its overall magic. And that this is how it is supposed to be.

This is how it was when the young Kutenai man, having purified himself with sweat baths, set out from his village toward a shining, tooth-shaped summit. He planned to stay atop that peak for many days. He would sit and pray and fast there until his special animal came to speak to him in a vision. If he was worthy, the spirit guide might transfer to him some of its power and tell him what he must do in his life.

The young man still was not sure which creature among the denizens of the mountainsides was the one that would speak to his heart. Some people seemed to know from an early age. But he had never felt that kind of affinity for one particular animal tribe. He was intrigued by them all. The elders told him not to worry; by the time he reached the summit, his guide would have given him a sign.

The prevailing winds that wash up against the northern Rockies come from the west, carrying Pacific air masses laden with moisture. Enough rain and snow fall on some sites to support habitats not very different from those of the Olympic Peninsula. At the base of the mountain, the young man found himself in a grove of cedar and hemlock with calypso orchids at their feet and a shadowed stream winding past the edge. He was looking for a good place to ford the current when he saw a dark grizzly coming toward him in the water. It was chasing spawning cutthroat across a shallow gravel bar. He experienced no twinge of fear upon beholding the bear, perhaps because he felt swept up in a sacred journey that was somehow greater than himself. Just the same, he found it strange. This had never happened to him before.

The next morning, he heard a strange squealing in the trees while breaking camp. Investigating, he found a fisher dragging away the porcupine it had just killed. Moving on, he considered how bold yet nimble this larger, darker cousin of the pine marten must be to overcome the porcupine's defenses and wondered if there was a lesson here for him.

By late afternoon, he was up in the bright realm of talus slopes and glacier lilies. He rested and watched a pika gather shed mountain goat fur for its burrow, then return to clip off sedges and penstemons and stack them in piles to dry in the sun. For some reason, he found each lightning-quick movement of this diminutive rock dweller absorbing, and he thought: Within that small rabbit-like body dwells a life force to match huge mountains, a war cry that carries across their stone faces, and the wisdom to store food far ahead of the winter. But his thoughts kept returning to the reflections of the bear he had seen rippling in the clear waters.

That evening, the seeker looked over a ridge to find a grizzly striding near a turquoise lake below a hanging glacier. The great bear was gold as fall aspen leaves. It caught his scent on the wind and halted and looked his way. The man found himself aware of every shade of evening light around him, every rock contour and each wisp of wind. Suddenly, the mountain bowl was ringing with messages for him. When the bear stood up and held its arms slightly out for balance, and the man was not frightened even then but felt instead that this was a gesture of beckoning, he knew. He knew the great bear was his guide and that in the days to come it would visit him with a true vision. Already it had taught him that a person can take hold of fear and use it to open his senses more keenly than ever to the beauty of the world.

There is something of the impulse to make a vision quest in every person because, from time to time, we all yearn to shake off the fetters of everyday existence and win a greater clarity and strength of purpose in our lives. There is nothing like mountains and the company of indomitable beasts to open your ears to the voices of nature. The young Kutenai has been gone a long time. But alpenglow still lights the summit, and grizzlies still wander by the lake in the basin just below. Somewhere between them, visions await, for they, too, are part of enduring America.

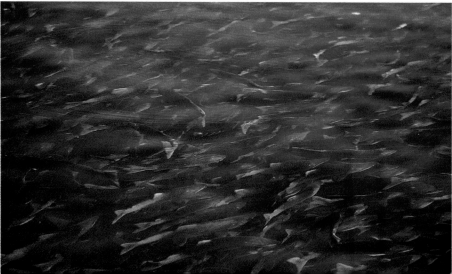

*S*almon and bear—linked in legend and in life—meet as they have for millennia. Sockeyes struggle upstream to spawn, fighting past eagles, otters, especially bears. Native Americans revered the fish, believing that, as all animals, it had an inner spirit. They marked its reappearance each year with First Salmon rituals.

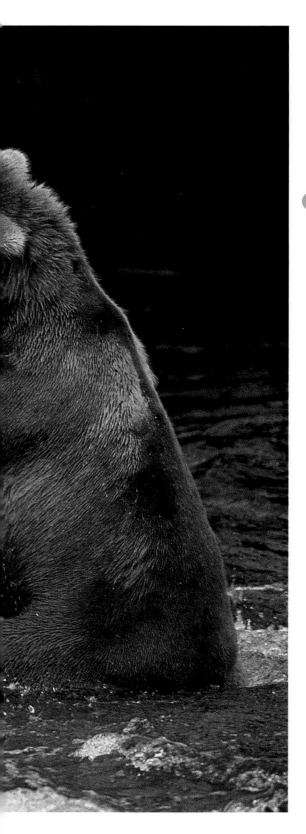

*S*almon-fishing bears
tend to tolerate each other's
presence, but battles, mock
or real, often erupt. These
two—ears back, mouths
open—may mean business.

*Following pages: In Alaska's
Icy Bay, glaciers calve year-
round. Inland lies Wrangell-
St. Elias National Park, a
wilderness of mountains, ice-
fields, and glaciers much like
the icebound North America
of two million years ago.*

*S*outheastern Alaska's coastal waters, rocky shores, intertidal zones, and sandy bottoms provide habitats for many creatures, among them sea urchins (above) and cockles and sea stars (right).

*M*osses, ferns, and waterfalls receive the benediction of a cool, humid climate in the rain forest of Washington's Olympic Peninsula. Behind a pair of raccoons, nurse logs— fallen trees—slowly decay, supporting and renewing life on the forest floor. Roosevelt elk roam the area, wintering on the peninsula's southwestern mountain slopes.

Sunset-tinged clouds obscure an Olympic Peninsula stream as it flows

past forests and ridges to mingle, in time, with the western sea.

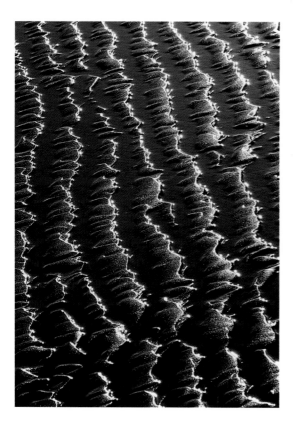

*W*here the Olympic Mountains tumble down to Lake Crescent, legend says, the spirit of Mount Storm King grew angry with battling Indians who broke the peace in his valley. Storm King hurled part of his crest, damming a river and creating the lake. To the west, flying gulls and sand riffles mark Pacific beaches.

*A*mong the oldest living things on earth, the great
sequoias of the Sierra Nevada have stood tall for centuries.
The General Grant (right), was a seedling during the life of
Christ, an era when many groups of Indians thrived here.

*H*abitat for mule deer and
Joshua trees, the Mojave Desert
(right), home to Paleo-Indians,
was cooler and wetter thousands
of years ago. Joshua trees have
grown here for 5,000 years.

Land of Salmon and Bear

*E*lephant seal pups and a mother sea otter with her pup live along the California coast. A Yurok legend tells how Thunder and Earthquake filled the ocean to give food to the people.

Preceding pages: The Pacific surf breaks against California's rocky shore at Point Lobos, a sanctuary for marine mammals.

*A*lone ponderosa pine stands in a frosty Yosemite National Park, where the crystal water of the Merced River reflects the sunlit, monolithic granite face of El Capitan.

Following pages: Against a backdrop of cardon cactus, a cirio—or boojum tree—grows in Baja California, habitat also of osprey, golden eagles, elephant seals, mountain lions, gray foxes, and other animals that range the Far West.

A THOUSAND YEARS AGO, INDIANS CARVED THESE ENIGMATIC FIGURES ON A ROCK WALL IN UTAH.

Land of Coyote and Hawk

*T*he storytellers say dust whirlwinds are caused by a bird flying
fast in a circle and crying out its loud song: Killdeer! Killdeer! *In
the hottest part of summer, when the air over the valleys shimmers
like a cooking fire and dust whirlwinds play in the dry lake beds,
most of the plants look brown and dead. But sagebrush, which
stays green all year and gives us medicine tea and bark for string
and sandals and makes shelter for the animals, sagebrush, which
laughs at every kind of weather, is just putting out its flowers. For
us, this is a sign that the pine nuts are forming high up in the
mountains. Scouting parties go to find where the cones are thickest
and throw dust in the air to chase away ghosts that could harm
the crop. The scouts gather some of the young, green nuts and one
small tree and bring them back down from the mountains to camp.
Then, as night falls, the Paiute people make a circle. Shoulder to
shoulder, they begin to dance round and round the pine tree,*

A darkling beetle navigates waves of gypsum sand beneath a

cloud-streaked sky in New Mexico's Tularosa Basin.

singing, always singing. They sing the songs everyone has learned. They sing the ones Man-Who-Knows-Many-Songs remembers and the ones owned by people who got them in a dream. The songs are very strong. With the dance, they have the power to bring rain and make sure the pine nuts keep growing.

A woman circles around the dancers in the opposite direction. Using a twig from the part of the sagebrush that is new and flowering, she takes water from her basket and shakes drops out over the ground. This, too, has the power to bring rain and many nuts. Next, the woman makes more circles, this time sprinkling the green pine nuts onto the ground, for whenever something is taken from the earth, something must be given back. It is why if you dig up a yampa root or yellow bell bulb you should put a pretty pebble in the hole, or just a stick. In the middle of the night, the dancers rest. Then they dance on until the People's Father, the sun, returns.

After the ceremony the Paiute go about their usual lives until the wild rose fruits in the valley turn red. That tells them the pine nuts are also ripe at last, and everyone will go to the mountains with big woven baskets and hopeful hearts. All the time they are there, they will be talking to the high country, asking it to give them good health and cool breezes for sleeping at night. Mostly, they are asking to take many pine nuts with them to keep hunger from the winter camp.

Sometimes even when the rains are good, the pine nuts are few. No one really knows why. Or why jackrabbits grow in number until there seems to be a long-ear under every bush, then become rare for years afterward. Or what makes the grasshoppers suddenly change shape one summer and fly together across the countryside like a dark storm. Maybe it is spirit business, as some say. Or the work of coyote, cleverest of the four-legged people; as the Trickster, he is always thinking up jokes to play. But maybe it is only the way of this part of the world.

The expanse between the West Coast Cascade and Sierra Nevada Ranges and the Rockies is often referred to as the intermountain West. This is the land of coyote and hawk, and it is the thirstiest part of the continent. The southern portion holds America's true deserts, which receive on average ten inches or less of rainfall per year. Driest, hottest, and lowest of all is part of the Mojave, where desert tortoises crawl among Joshua trees and creosote bushes in the rain shadow of the Sierra Nevada, and Death Valley actually dips below sea level. To the east and south is the Sonoran Desert, distinguished by its cactus forests of saguaro and cholla. Still farther east and south, roadrunners chase lizards among mesquite and grasses in the Chihuahuan Desert of New Mexico, Texas, and Mexico.

The rest of the intermountain West is considerably higher. Standing 4,000 feet or more above sea level, it is watered by 8 to 12 inches of annual precipitation. Most of that comes as snow, for while summers are nearly as hot as in the true deserts, winter brings subzero temperatures and white-out blizzards. Some refer to this realm of extremes as the cold desert, or the shrub steppe. A lot of people just call it sagebrush country.

The hardy bush that scientists label *Artemisia* can be found in cool drylands throughout the world. North America has about a dozen different woody species of sagebrush with at least 18 subspecies between them. Together, they dominate parts of the Columbia and Colorado Plateaus, the Wyoming Basin, and an even grander sweep of mostly unfenced terrain—the Great Basin, which takes in western Utah, parts of southern Oregon and southern Idaho, and the bulk of Nevada.

The waters of the Great Basin have no outlet to the sea. They collect in countless little pools and a few bigger bodies, most notably Great Salt Lake. Then they evaporate, leaving minerals to concentrate as salts and alkali deposits. The Great Basin contains 90 separate basins amid more than 160 distinct mountain ranges thrust up by the same forces that elevated the Cascade and Sierra Nevada chains along the coast. Peaks 10,000 to 13,000 feet tall rise in the heart of the somewhat misleadingly named intermountain West. Some biologists think the most abundant ungulate of this region, about the year 1200, may have been bighorn sheep.

As dawn reaches over the shoulder of

Desert West

a snowbound crag in eastern Nevada, a pair of coyotes are picking a route along some cliffs farther down. It is early spring. The bighorns have descended from their usual range to graze the first green sprouts appearing on the lower slopes. After coming upon a group of females and subadults, the coyotes gave chase, trying to cut off one of the small yearlings. The sheep outmaneuvered them easily on the rocky terrain.

As the coyotes followed along a narrow trail, their shoulders brushed an overhanging rock face with images of bighorns etched into it. With them were coiled serpents—probably rattlesnakes—also by the hand of Paiute hunters from an otherwise forgotten century. The coyotes' attention stayed fixed upon their footing until their noses caught a new scent. They followed it to a solitary old ewe lying in a partial cave. Carrying an infestation of lungworms aggravated by a heavy winter, she had been able to struggle this far with the herd but could no longer keep up. She rose at the coyotes' approach and started to totter away. They had her down within a few steps.

The pair fed on the meat for several days, eventually taking turns with golden eagles and a Swainson's hawk. Small groups of ravens arrived to join them. One or two of the talkative, black birds were bold enough to pull the hawk's tailfeathers with their beaks, distracting the raptor long enough to let them hop onto a choice part of the carcass for a bite. Magpies uncovered many of the scraps the ravens cached close by. Sage sparrows and sage thrashers picked up some of the scattered wool for nest lining. White-tailed antelope squirrels did the same during the day. At night, desert woodrats hauled more wool and part of the hoofs and horns back to their stick nests in crevices among the cliffs.

Now, having spent the night picking over the last remains, the coyotes are departing for a marshy alkali lake in the valley bottom. Waterfowl are beginning to arrive in big flocks, and other prey will be coming to drink as the days continue to warm. The song-dogs have another reason to visit the lake. Next to it is a hill with loose digging soil on the edge of a sheltered ravine. The female has denned there for the past two years, and she is once again heavy with pups.

On a broad alluvial fan leading out from the mountain's base, the female stops in mid-stride and stares intently toward the east. She cocks her ears forward. Her tail lifts straight out behind her with excitement. Giving a quick glance over at the male, she leads toward the source, pausing every so often to listen, gradually assuming more of a crouch.

Land of Coyote and Hawk

In the distance, glowing like fat thistles in the early light, are the largest of American grouse—sage grouse, scores of them. The males gather where the sagebrush gives way to clumps of lupine, long-leaved phlox, and bare, rocky ground. They have been coming since the earliest dawn light every morning for weeks to strut back and forth in the clearing, wings quivering and their stiff, pointed tail feathers spread into a fan. Closer up, from where the coyotes have positioned themselves behind a screen of rabbit brush, the white, velvety plumage on the front of the males draws attention each time the chest is inflated by underlying air sacs. The chest is further embellished with twin golden patches of bare skin to match the showy gold feather ridge above each eye, while the air sacs produce booming, popping, and whistling noises.

It seems an impressive display by almost any species' standards. Yet the hens drawn to this strutting ground, known as a lek, are attracted to the cocks as part of complex behavioral patterns. The cocks divide their efforts between courting incoming females and keeping competitors at bay, occasionally advancing from a puffed-up threat to a wing-beating attack. Dominant males may win a mating territory near the lek's center.

Silently, the coyotes separate and begin to work around to opposite sides of the lek. But when the male pauses to survey the birds again, he fails to detect a single one. Curiosity soon draws him out from behind the branches for a better view. What he does not know is that the grouse have already spied his mate and lie crouched in the shadows. And when he appears toward the opposite side, the clearing erupts with a whir of wings. The explosion flushes a jackrabbit from the base of a sagebrush where it had been feeding on newly sprouted Idaho fescue and bluebunch wheatgrass. The male coyote rushes after it but cannot match its zigzag course through the scrub and gives up that hunt as well.

The grouse disperse and begin their morning feeding, pecking at a variety of buds and sagebrush leaves. Resting at the base of another sagebrush next to the tunnels of Ord's kangaroo rats, the jackrabbit listens carefully with swiveling ears—desert-dweller's ears. Long, thin, and suffused with blood vessels close to the surface, they serve as much to dissipate heat in the hottest months as to gather sound. As for the coyotes, they touch noses briefly after reuniting, then continue on toward the lake through the endless, silvery green sagebrush sea.

The perennially green leaves of sagebrush, coupled with a massive root system, give it a head start on the growing season. By the time competing vegetation is putting forth its first shoots, typical sagebrush is already growing an extra set of elongated leaves to harvest the sunlight. Then, as the other plants struggle to cope with the rising heat of summer, sagebrush drops those long leaves, called ephemerals, to help conserve moisture. The fine hairs that give sagebrush its silver sheen help protect the remaining leaves by slowing evaporation and reflecting sunlight. Volatile oils responsible for the bush's unmistakable, bittersweet tang guard the leaves as well by making them indigestible to most animals.

Sage grouse are one exception, relying almost exclusively on sagebrush leaves through the winter. Black-tailed jackrabbits are another. The fact that sagebrush serves them as a virtually limitless food supply figures in the population's tendency to increase to astonishing levels before overcrowding, stress, and disease lead to a crash. Jackrabbits were a main source of protein for many Paiute bands, who often organized drives to capture the hares in nets. The Indians preferred the taste of white-tailed jackrabbits, which themselves prefer grasses and herbs, as do the region's cottontail rabbits and unique pygmy rabbits. Although mule deer will nibble some of sagebrush's new growth in spring, pronghorns are the only native ungulate that can eat *Artemisia* in any quantity. After about 1200, the land of coyote and hawk never included big herds of larger-bodied grazers such as bison and elk. It could not support them.

The Great Basin held the territories of the Shoshone, the Gosiute, and the Ute as well as the Paiute, who lived scattered in relatively small family bands. Some had close ties to certain lakes, where they took spawning fish, migrating ducks, and cattails. Even so, every group still spent much of the year on the move between a variety of foods. The Paiute collected about 40 kinds of seeds, including Indian ricegrass, Great Basin wild rye, and the crucial autumn supply of pine nuts. They collected ant eggs as well and, like the area's horned larks and western bluebirds, picked grasshoppers from plants early in the morning before the night's chill wore off.

Because of their mobility, the Paiute used only rudimentary shelters. They dressed in rabbit pelts in winter and little or nothing through the warm months. They never mastered the horse. They were an essentially intact Stone Age hunter-gatherer culture, one splendidly attuned to, and in balance with, a harsh, spare environment where—evidence suggests— they and their forerunners successfully lived for at least 10,000 years.

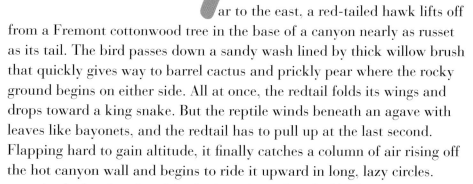

ar to the east, a red-tailed hawk lifts off from a Fremont cottonwood tree in the base of a canyon nearly as russet as its tail. The bird passes down a sandy wash lined by thick willow brush that quickly gives way to barrel cactus and prickly pear where the rocky ground begins on either side. All at once, the redtail folds its wings and drops toward a king snake. But the reptile winds beneath an agave with leaves like bayonets, and the redtail has to pull up at the last second. Flapping hard to gain altitude, it finally catches a column of air rising off the hot canyon wall and begins to ride it upward in long, lazy circles.

As the hawk gains altitude, it notices a band of bighorn rams grazing blackbrush on a gravelly bench in a side canyon. They are desert bighorns, with thinner horns than the subspecies found in the northern intermountain West and Rockies. Soaring still higher, the hawk escapes the main gorge and wheels across a much wider bench stippled with saltbush and sagebrush. Once again, it drops like a spear. And this time, the redtail comes up with a western collared lizard, which had been raising and lowering the front of its body in a territorial display for a rival.

The hawk rests just long enough to tear the lizard into pieces it can swallow, then flies on to the far end of the benchland, where the red sandstone layers of the canyon side reappear. Catching another thermal, the bird rises along with them. Having moved through habitats with elements from the Sonoran Desert and then sagebrush country, the hawk is soon gliding past slopes where the sagebrush mingles with piñon and juniper. Farther up, on the canyon rim, where white-throated swifts trace high-speed lacework patterns through the upwelling air, those conifers in turn join ponderosa pine, gambel oak, and scattered groves of aspen.

Before it gets to the rim, the hawk veers off to follow an offshoot valley toward a particular cliff where a section of rock partway up the face has been weathered away to create a massive overhang. At the base of that natural roof is a crowded colony of creatures. Human creatures. They hail the hawk when it approaches. Their huge, hive-like dwelling is fashioned of poles and sandstone blocks with hundreds of separate rooms and underground chambers for storing grain and performing ceremonies. What the redtail makes of the place and its inhabitants is hard to guess. Its main interest lies at the cliff's base. The hawk has seldom failed to find rodents scurrying there among the heaps of refuse and spilled grain.

The high, semidesert country where Colorado, Utah, Arizona, and New Mexico come together falls within the geographic province called the Colorado Plateau, perhaps better known as America's canyonlands. The area's sedimentary strata were formed during the Mesozoic era under conditions that strongly oxidized their iron content. The result, once uplifted in a titanic block, was thousands of vertical feet of rust-colored stone; some orange, some pink, and some a vermilion vivid as the hedgehog cactus flowers blooming in cracks on hot ledges. Water then cut sharply and deeply into the layers, fashioning the canyon country's extraordinary architecture of mesas and chasms, with some layers pared down to free-standing towers, fins, and pinnacles. Here and there, frost is still working them into balancing boulders and arches.

We can no longer see everything that the redtail saw as it soared through this landscape centuries ago. Not even the first Navajos who arrived on the Colorado Plateau around 1500 encountered the cliff dwellers. Like us, they found only abandoned ruins with the dry wind gusting through them, and they gave the vanished inhabitants the name Anasazi—ancient ones.

The early Anasazi are thought to have pursued a hunting and seed-gathering lifestyle much like that of the neighboring Paiute, whose range extended to the western edge of the Colorado Plateau. Being higher and wetter than most of the intermountain West, the plateau offered more forests bearing pine nuts and acorns, more deer, and more potential for growing crops. The Anasazi began to supplement their foraging with cultivated maize and pumpkins. Over time, they added beans, squash, and other vegetables to their diet. They also added turkeys that either they or another Southwest tribe domesticated from a native subspecies. Through trade and plunder, the tame turkeys would eventually make their way south to the Aztec empire in Mexico. Conquistador Hernán Cortés later appropriated some and shipped them home to Europe. From there, farmyard turkeys traveled back to the New World with colonists of the East Coast. All the domestic varieties throughout the world today are descended from the wild turkeys originally tamed nearly two millennia ago in North America's drylands.

It is autumn now in this sculpted stone portion of the land of coyote and hawk. The trembling of aspen leaves in a wind washing over the rimrock fills the afternoon with coruscating gold light. Western tanagers with yellow sides and red heads fly between the branches. Tassel-eared squirrels and Steller's jays gather acorns below the orange-turning oaks while Clark's nutcrackers and piñon jays harvest the pine nut crop once shared with the Anasazi. Like both the Indians and the squirrels, the nutcrackers and jays store most of this bounty to see them through leaner times.

Carrying as many as a hundred piñon nuts at once in a pouch beneath its tongue, a nutcracker may cache between 20,000 and 33,000 before the season is through. And it must recover seeds from upward of 1,000 of its cache sites—all located by memory with the help of landmarks such as rocks—if it is to stay in good condition until the spring breeding season. The piñon jay is usually able to begin breeding in late winter, somewhat earlier than many of its competitors, because it has so much food readily available in nut caches for both itself and its young. If the late summer and fall brings a bumper crop, this will stimulate the piñon jays to begin breeding right away.

Scrub jays may come from their brushier habitats at lower elevations to join in the harvest, and they, too, cache quantities of nuts. The combined effort of these birds, acorn woodpeckers, and various squirrels removes an enormous number of the seeds put forth by the piñons to reproduce themselves. Yet since most of the caches are on the ground, they also feed black bears that happen upon them and rodents, from long-tailed voles to golden-mantled ground squirrels. Equally important, for all the cache owners' memorization skills and the scavengers' searching abilities, a great many seed troves are never recovered. Dug into the ground and covered over, they are effectively planted and will soon yield seedlings, continually regenerating the piñon forest.

A red-tailed hawk dives off the top of a ponderosa snag leaning out over the canyon edge, then flares its wings out over the abyss. It no sooner levels off than it begins to dive again and, tucking one wing close to its body, performs a series of corkscrew spirals straight downward. Normally, such behavior is reserved for courtship and territorial displays. Why this bird is performing is an open question. Maybe the answer is: because it can.

Later, in its descent toward the desert floor of the canyon, the hawk passes by an old cliff dwelling. There is no sign of life among the crumbling adobe bricks. But there are faint prints in the dust, and they look fresh. They belong to a mountain lion that sometimes uses the cave area as a resting spot between hunts. In an underground chamber where pottery fragments litter the floor, the little-known, nocturnal raccoon relative called the ringtail sleeps, awaiting the coming of dusk.

Archaeologists think the Anasazi abandoned their homeland in the face of prolonged and serious drought sometime during the 13th century. Their descendants live to the south and east. These are the Pueblo and Hopi Indians, who continue the agricultural traditions and ceremonies of the ancient ones. Hopi villages still include the underground chambers called kivas, which represent the hole in the ground through which people emerged to live in the world. Three times, the stories say, humanity has come into being, and three times the world order has been completely destroyed because people ceased to honor the creator's divine laws. As the hawk continues down the cliff faces, it reaches a stratum laden with fossils representing the era of the dinosaurs. In many experts' view, dinosaurs never really went extinct. Small ones, whose scales were modified into feathers, can be seen almost anywhere you look.

The redtail steepens its angle of descent and hurtles down toward the basement of time. Sunset is approaching, and the rust-bright canyon walls take on even deeper colors. But they bear the same message as always, which is that the history of life contains both more change and more continuity than most of us will ever be able to fathom.

STAR TRAILS ARC ABOVE WEATHERED ROCK FORMATIONS OF UTAH'S CANYON COUNTRY.

*D*eep in Grand Canyon, Havasu Falls cascades into a blue-green pool. A mineral-tinted rock painting and rock-cut granaries testify to centuries of Indian life in the canyon.

Following pages: An instant's slender flash of lightning leaps from clouds toward millions of years of Grand Canyon strata.

*T*he Arizona desert shows its moods in the spiny, stately saguaro, the blur of golden poppies, and a wealth of blue lupines, orange globe mallows, and other native springtime wildflowers.

*S*un warms a red-rock crevice and a rock-red desert spiny lizard.

Diurnal lizards change skin color during the day, reflecting the sun's rays.

*S*acred ethereal rock art and mountain peaks mark the lands where the Anasazi built dwellings that were part of the sheltering sandstone cliffs and their earth mother herself. Saguaros spike the Sonoran Desert.

Following pages: A golden dawn rises beyond Mesa Arch on the slickrock wilderness of the Utah desert.

*E*ons of erosion by water, frost, and windblown sand
sculptured the fins, arches, spires, and canyons of the Colorado Plateau. Delicate Arch, Junction Butte, and White
Rim sandstone-capped pillars stand in southeastern Utah,
along with the country's greatest concentration of canyons.

Land of Coyote and Hawk

Where the coyote prowls sagebrush flats on the hunt for prey, hawks search from above—the resident redtail (soaring) and the migratory Swainson's. Indian legend says that the coyote, so clever and adaptable, will be the last animal on earth.

*B*oth nature and human beings form the desert. Winds shape and reshape sand dunes in an area of Colorado revered as a cradle of ancestral Pueblo peoples. Nearby, these Anasazi—the Hovenweep people—built straight-walled stone masonry dwellings.

Low clouds and late-day shadows spread across Colorado scrubland

below snowcapped peaks of the San Juan Mountains.

*O*n the wild, stark landscape of West Texas, stand the
nation's southernmost mountain ranges—the Chisos, with
the desert's spiky native agave, and the Guadalupes (opposite), part of a 250-million-year-old fossil reef.

n the Mexican state of Sonora, pink hedgehog cactuses and teddy bear chollas brighten an ancient lava bed. Morning sunlight creates a sparkling rainbow where Basaséachic Falls plunges some 800 feet to a pool in Chihuahua state's Copper Canyon.

*T*he skeleton of an ancient volcano, New Mexico's Ship Rock is sacred to

the Navajo, who call it tse bit'a'i—*the rock with wings.*

Land of Coyote and Hawk

Sanctuaries along the Rio Grande give refuge to sandhill cranes and coots (below) and great flocks of snow geese.

Following pages: The ladder that rises from an Anasazi kiva—a sacred underground chamber—evokes the emergence of Pueblo ancestors from their primordial home deep in their earth mother.

A RITUAL INVOCATION TO THE BUFFALO EVOKES ITS ROLE AS SYMBOL OF THE GREAT PLAINS.

Land of Pronghorn and Bison

Even before there was a beginning, there was Inyan, who was without form or substance but was everywhere and all-powerful. The powers lay in his blood, and his blood was blue. Wishing others to exist, Inyan set about making them from parts of his own body. He took so much of himself that the blood all spilled out from him. It became the waters upon the first thing he had created—the great disk Maka, our mother, the earth. Maka arranged this beautiful blue color into rivers and lakes and little ponds to ornament herself. The powers could not live in water, however, and they soon left. But you can see them every time you look up, for they formed the great blue dome over Maka that we call the sky. So say the Lakota Sioux.

The nations of the Sioux live between the earth and the huge blue sky in the heart of the continent, which is made of grass. Their legends hold that, in the early days of the world, the Buffalo

A buffalo—or American bison—pauses at sunset against a sweep of

South Dakota's Badlands, part of a range it has occupied since the Ice Age.

People, as bison were known, lived underground and served the great beings in the spirit world. Then the Buffalo People emerged from a hole in the earth and spread across the land. They came in order to provide humans with meat and fat; hides for robes, tipis, medicine bundles, and drums; sinews for lashings and bowstrings; bones for tools, decoration, and ceremonial pipes; in short, with nearly everything they needed.

Modern science says the bison came, like most of the New World's large mammals, from Eurasian ancestors that crossed the Bering Land Bridge during the Ice Age. But the true strength and fabulous abundance of the American bison, often called buffalo, really did well up from underground. They arose from the deep, incredibly fertile soils—prairy-erths—that nourished the roots of the largest expanse of grasslands on earth. Consisting of western shortgrass, eastern tallgrass, and midland mixed grass portions, the Great Plains, the land of pronghorn and bison, rolled across one of every nine acres on the continent.

People tend to envision the Plains Indians as cultures on horseback, traveling those grand open spaces atop painted ponies and running down buffalo at full gallop. Yet from the end of the Ice Age until the arrival of Spanish conquistadors, there was not a horse to be had on the continent. The tribes traveled afoot with camp dogs dragging supplies in travois. To get close enough to kill game in this exposed habitat called for extra measures of stealth and patience. Hunters often concealed themselves beneath buffalo hides. In certain places, one would try to mingle with a herd and get them moving in the direction he chose. If they followed, this decoy—called a buffalo runner—would pick up speed until the herd was racing behind him. At the last minute, he would dodge to safety while other hunters closed in from the sides and rear to funnel the panicked animals onward toward a cliff. Then humps and tongues and sweet backstrap meat for all would rain upon the rocks below.

Some people might haul a bleached skull from an earlier drive back to camp as well. This part of the bison served as a symbol of the herds and a kind of conduit for transferring their power to humans. One painted with sacred designs rested next to the hearth in the center of Sioux tipis. As a test of their resolve and a plea for a boon from the spir-its, Cheyenne warriors might attach a string of bison skulls to bone pins skewering their back and then march about the camp dragging the heavy, horned weights behind them. The Mandan wrapped their dead in buffalo robes and placed them on platforms, feet toward the rising sun. Later, they would set each skull nearby on the ground to join others in a ring around those of bison. In death, as in life, the buffalo and the people formed one great circle.

Seen from a distance, they resemble boulders inexplicably heaved up out of the flatness. Closer up, brown eyes stare back from deep within tangles of coiled wool while sunlit horns curve round to frame the bearded face, somewhat like a halo. Most of the animals' bulk appears thrust forward into those shaggy heads and forequarters. The flanks look slender and naked by comparison, as if, like the Minotaur, they are half cloven-hoofed beast, half human. Or Buffalo People.

There are four of them, all bulls. There used to be five. But the fifth, the dominant leader of this male band, died during the night, worn out by the years and one last, long winter of shoveling aside snows and icy crusts with his heavy head to get at the grasses buried underneath. He lies motionless now on the new sprouts of spring. For a while, the other bulls would nudge him with their horns as if trying to get his attention or, perhaps, lift him back onto his feet. They still chase off the coyotes drawn to the carcass and magpies swooping in to peck at the eyes. And every so often, the bulls will slowly circle the body together, plodding round and round, swinging their heads. What such behavior means to the Buffalo People is their secret. It may mean nothing at all. Maybe the movement only looks portentous to us, who have invented so many ceremonies in the hope of persuading fate to tilt a little in our favor.

West of the dead bull and his four attendants, where a game trail leads past a lone box elder tree, lies a shallow depression. A mere dimple in the sweep of countryside, it stands out mostly because the rest is so level. This miniature landform arose because a badger once dug a thirteen-lined ground squirrel from its burrow here. A bison then spread the heap of excavated dirt around with its hoofs

Great Plains

and lay down in the center to dust bathe, coating the hair and hide to help ward off biting bugs. The animal's pawing and rolling enlarged the bare spot, which later attracted other bison for dust bathing. After a heavy rain, still more came to wallow in the mud, and the depression kept growing until the herd finally moved on.

Generations have passed since then. Vegetation long ago reclaimed the scraped and trampled soil. Yet while grasses and wildflowers flourish on all sides, the old wallow has rushes growing in its center and sedges toward its rim. These water-loving plants can make a home here because the low spot becomes a temporary pond as winter snows melt and again during summer cloudbursts. Toads and tiger salamanders have come to depend upon the site for breeding. So have a variety of insects and smaller life forms. Killdeer and long-billed curlews probe the edges for aquatic larvae, and bigger creatures such as these bison bulls pause in their travels to sip. You see, even as we keep trying to influence fate with charms and ceremonies, we are surrounded by miracles that happen of their own accord. Mix together a little dirt and a little water in the middle of an ordinary prairie, and you get fairy shrimp, tadpoles changing into golden-eyed land-walkers, plover cries, and looming reflections of buffalo past and present.

The immense, wild pastures of the Great Plains supported, along with some 60 million bison, an almost equal number of pronghorns. They also held millions of mule deer and more millions of elk, originally more a creature of the plains than of the mountains. And the biomass— the sheer living weight—of all these prairie herds was probably matched or exceeded by the multitudes of smaller grazers, including ground squirrels, marmots, pocket gophers, and an estimated 5 billion prairie dogs.

Now imagine the predators thriving upon this panorama of protein. You could start with the plains grizzly, known to the Lakota as Hu Nonp. He once stood up on his hind legs, as bears will, and danced before the great spirits. He taught them how to play the drums and make music and songs. The spirits passed these arts on to humans and rewarded Hu Nonp by designating him the keeper of wisdom and medicine and the protector of shamans. In Indian times, the bear population was so large and genetically varied that the plains were inhabited not only by typical brown grizzlies with silver-tipped fur but also by black, white, gold, reddish, and piebald grizzlies.

Imagine alongside these great, intelligent bears of many hues hundreds upon hundreds of thousands of plains wolves. Imagine their songs traveling in the restless prairie winds while thunderstorms stampeded across the sky. Then imagine with them coyotes, red foxes, and the member of the canine family most closely tied to American grasslands: swift foxes. Then the badgers and black-footed ferrets and long-tailed weasels that also hunted the little grazers. Then ferruginous hawks—the largest hawks on the continent—and northern harriers soaring by, scattering meadowlarks, bobolinks, and prairie chickens. And waterfowl. Half the continent's ducks reared their young on prairie pothole lakes—Maka's blue ornaments, shining like polished beadwork in the sun. Imagine all the wings, hoofs, paws, and voices moving together out on that meeting place of the sod and the sky. Lastly, imagine yourself moving among them.

The spectacle around you represents only about one third of the true grassland community, the transitory part. Drought can wither it. Wildfire can sweep through and turn every stalk to ash. Yet the prairie will spring back time and again from its stronghold—the densely interlaced, questing tangle of roots and root hairs that extend 10 and 15 feet down into loamy darkness.

If strung out as a single line, the webwork beneath one square yard of tallgrass would run for 20 miles. A single cubic foot of such sod harbors roughly a million of the small roundworms known as nematodes. Their ranks include grazers, hunters, and scavengers, and they live within a community that includes similarly astonishing numbers of common earthworms, mites, insect larvae, and harvester ants. When each generation of grasses dies, the tissues, mixed with the husks and droppings of creatures small and large, are soon reduced to particles by these subterranean herds. A combination of microbes and fungi works the residue into clumps with carbon stored in the center, transforming plain dirt into a mass of tiny, organic granules.

As the soils create the living grasslands, so the grasslands create more living soils. For millennium upon millennium, both grew ever thicker and more fertile. And then, so suddenly that in terms of geologic time it was as if a meteor had struck the Great Plains, both the Indian cultures and the throngs of wildlife were devastated. Those boundless expanses of rippling grass that explorers kept comparing to the sea were cut into small, square plots, where the sod was ripped to shreds and seeded with domestic grains.

The wealth of carbon and other nutrients banked in the prairyerths was still there; it would feed the emerging nations of the United States and Canada and much of the rest of the world besides. But the domain of pronghorn and bison, plains grizzly and black-footed ferret, was overwhelmed in the process. What used to be the most characteristic of America's wild landscapes stands today as the most fragmented and incomplete. No park or refuge to protect a truly representative sample of this ecosystem's flora and fauna was ever set aside.

Here, then, is the one major region, and the one chapter of this book, in which we cannot rediscover our wild heritage by exploring special places where it endures essentially intact. There are none. But if we try, we can find enough threads of the original heartland to help us weave some of the old wholeness back together in our minds.

Like Theodore Roosevelt National Park in North Dakota and the newly established Grasslands National Park in southern Saskatchewan, Canada, South Dakota's Badlands National Park does not really encompass typical rolling prairie. It covers the breaks in between. The smooth surface of the plain disintegrates into a jumble of multicolored fins and spires with the bones of prehistoric giants sticking out of them. The Lakota saw this strange, eroded landscape as the resting place of a race of monsters destroyed by thunderbolts. Settlers found it too rugged to plow or even to make much use of for livestock grazing. As a result, there was room left for wildlife. Some species survived on their own, hidden among the folds and fossils. Others, such as the bison and, more recently, the swift fox, were brought in from surviving groups elsewhere.

Badlands Park includes the largest protected roadless area left on the American prairie, the Sage Creek Wilderness. It is only about 64,000 acres in size, smaller than some Western ranches. But it is enough to embrace you on a long ramble across the bottom of the sky. You pick a point on the horizon and navigate toward it over treeless swells with the wind at your shoulder for company. The miles pass, and yet the horizon comes no closer. If anything, it seems to be forever opening around you, drawing you out toward the four sacred directions recognized by the Indians. You begin to feel like smoke drifting through the buffalo grass; through the wheatgrass and little bluestem, the Junegrass, needle-and-thread, ricegrass, and side oats grama; through the wild prairie roses and yellow coneflowers and the scarlet globe mallows. Pronghorns the color of last year's sun-cured stalks gust by in the distance, while meadowlarks call out a song on the wing that is like day breaking all over again.

Before long, another pronghorn rounds a low rise. It is a female, grazing a patch of star lilies. Not far away from her, a bobcat pads up from the chokecherry brush in a gully. The doe flares her cloud-white rump patches, emitting a sweet, almondine musk, and begins to run. Yet instead of racing away, she makes a fast arc that brings her around to within 40 feet of the cat.

The pronghorn—sometimes called antelope—is the only large, hoofed animal in North America whose line arose on this continent rather than from Eurasian stock. It is the only ungulate in the world that possesses horns like those of bison or Africa's true antelope, yet sheds them each year, as do deer. But what really sets this beast apart is its speed. *Antilocapra americana* masters the ground the way the prairie falcons overhead master the air. Aided by an exceptionally large windpipe leading to oversize lungs, the pronghorn can move at close to 70 miles an hour, at which point it is covering as much as 20 feet at a bound. It can keep up a pace of at least 30 miles an hour for 15 miles. To understand why it would need to, you have to mentally weave the wolf back into the fabric of survival, or, rather, wolf packs, with individuals taking turns chasing their quarry in a kind of relay hunt.

Pronghorns commonly approach coyotes or bobcats and literally run circles around them. It may be their way of keeping the predators in plain view, removing any opportunity for a stalk. This particular female seems to be more interested in distracting the cat or perhaps leading it off in a different direction. Although she herself is at little risk of becoming a meal, it is early June, which means she may have other concerns.

If you follow her at a distance after the bobcat leaves, you might see the doe eventually make her way into a swale, where a pale fawn rises from the grass and slips beneath her flank to nurse. Finished, the infant races around her side for a while, exercising its spindly, fast-developing legs before vanishing again among the stalks. The mother moves on around a slight hill toward a stretch of low-growing vegetation pocked with conical mounds. While her baby waits alone and motionless for her return, she is about to join the busiest, most varied community on the plains: a prairie dog town.

During Indian times, these sociable, burrowing rodents fashioned not only towns but the occasional megalopolis. One covered an area larger than modern-day Los Angeles. Relentless poisoning cut the total of all four native prairie dog species by 90 percent or more and continues today. Stockmen insist that prairie dogs seriously compete with cattle. In reality, the rodents take only about 7 percent of the forage on typical prairie range.

Meanwhile, their activities—digging and cropping down vegetation for a better view around burrows—encourage the growth of new grass shoots and an assortment of herbs. Since these offer more protein than ordinary pastures, livestock actually seek out prairie dog towns for grazing through spring and early summer. Native ungulates always did. The mother pronghorn soon finds herself alongside mule deer and a group of bison with buffalo birds—now called cowbirds—perched upon their backs.

A golden eagle tacks by into the wind, perhaps looking for unwary young prairie dogs as they romp after one another and wrestle together in puppy-like heaps. But an older animal keeping watch gives off the sharp, high whistle that warns of hunters on the wing—one of a dozen different calls in the black-tailed prairie dog's repertoire. Instantly, the colony disappears underground. Silence reigns until two young bison bulls begin a head-shoving contest, grunting and pounding the ground with their hoofs as they struggle for footing. Shortly afterward, the first prairie dog peers out of its hole and issues an all-clear bark, and the bustle of hundreds of small bodies resumes.

What we can't see is the activity that continues beneath the surface. As ever, the life of the prairie gets only thicker and more diverse underground. Down in the dogs' labyrinthine network of tunnels, listening posts, turning bays, nest chambers, toilet chambers, and escape routes, small creatures from cottontail rabbits and harvest mice to crickets and spiders also find a home. Like the plants' root systems, they are sheltered here from midsummer heat and winter blizzards alike. The shaded, relatively moist environment is even more critical for amphibians such as the Great Plains toads that venture forth to breed in rain-filled buffalo wallows. Box turtles emerge from the burrows in the morning to bask in the sun and warm up before setting off to feast on insects, often breaking apart old bison droppings to get at dung beetles and grubs.

With one special organ in the roof of the mouth to analyze scents gathered by the flickering tongue and two more in pits—one on each side of its face—for detecting infrared waves from warm-blooded bodies, a rattlesnake in search of prey glides easily through the earthen tubes. The prairie dogs scurry ahead to dig fresh dirt from the walls and hammer it with their noses into a tightly packed plug. The rattler may stay on to rest for a while, safe from the raptors that hunt it. Many more of these reptiles may arrive during fall to hibernate together in big, slithering piles.

A number of tunnels are taken over by burrowing owls, which rear their young in them. Presumably, dog town predators such as swift foxes and badgers find it as hard as humans do to tell the warning rattle of a snake from the hiss young burrowing owls make when disturbed. Counting mountain plovers, upland sandpipers, horned larks, and other birds that like to forage where there is less high grass to hide possible danger, the pronghorn is one of more than 130 different kinds of vertebrates linked to black-tailed prairie dog colonies.

In the easternmost reaches of the Great Plains rise the most impressive grasslands of all, so sweet and green and thick and high that people on foot become lost within them. These are the tallgrass prairies. Watered by heavier precipitation than falls farther west in the long rain shadow of the Rockies, the ripe, black soils grow Indian grass, switchgrass, and, especially, big bluestem, five to twelve feet in height. They grow compass plant, a sunflower every inch as tall; the Omaha and Ponca used it in medicines, while settlers relied upon the leaves' north-south alignment to find their way through the towering meadows. They grow cat's claw sensitive brier, whose leaves fold at the touch. They grow heart-leaved golden alexander and blazing star, downy gentian and buffalo gourd. In all, they grow an untamed garden in which at least a dozen new flower species blossom every week from early spring through fall and butterflies of every kind color the air in between with petal-like wings.

et the list of spots where a visitor can find a good-size tract of these ultimate pastures and large native animals to go with them is brief: the Nature Conservancy's Tallgrass Prairie Preserve in Oklahoma and, farther north in the Kansas part of the Flint Hills, the Konza Prairie Research Natural Area. Two national wildlife refuges—Wichita Mountains in Oklahoma and Fort Niobrara in Nebraska—could be added, though much of their range consists of shorter, midsize grasses. And that's about it. Only a fraction of one percent of North America's original tallgrass prairie remains intact, and we must animate the majority of that almost entirely with our imaginings.

What is missing is not merely individual species but any semblance of the pageantry of animal empires arrayed upon the plains and the continual drama of interactions between them. Missing, too, is a sense of the great, free, migratory pulse of life within the prairie realm. A buffalo herd confined to a fenced refuge is an altogether different biological entity than a throng the length of a range of hills rumbling from Kansas to Montana and into Canada, urged on by ancient, inborn memories, patterns of rainfall and wildfire, the succession of plant growth, and forays by the wolves and bears patrolling the herd's fringes. In the end, we lose sight of how dynamic nature is and, thus, of how to save it. Ecosystems are all flux and flow, with natural selection—the shaping of fleetness, endurance, alertness, majesty—operating on a scale that simply cannot be re-created inside the confines of any one tiny, isolated reserve.

But wait. There is a big form moving among the tallgrass in a prairie plot where the most imposing mammals seen for years have been the marmots usually called woodchucks or groundhogs. The form is a human one, kneeling to inspect something. It is a woman, possibly white, possibly Indian. It is hard to tell from this distance, and even after you meet, you find it difficult to be sure.

As it turns out, she belongs to a group that has been working to restore this long-abandoned farmer's field. At first, they brought in native grasses and wildflowers by transplanting plugs of sod from frontier cemeteries and roadside ditches where some of the original flora survived. In later years, they were able to gather seeds from the first plants and sow them toward the outer edges. The spreading prairie vegetation itself soon transformed the hard-packed soil of the field into soft, lively earth. Native rodents moved in and worked the ground further through their tunneling, and the area began to attract hawks, weasels, and a badger no one knew was around.

The group started burning the plot at intervals to imitate lightning-sparked fires, a fundamental force in maintaining the vigor of tallgrasses and keeping woody invaders at bay. Already, the prairie is at a stage where this woman and her fellow volunteers want to bring a few bison and elk back into the equation. The dream, she says, is to restore not merely the look of a real prairie but the function. They are therefore contemplating ways to link this small piece to another a short distance away and then connect that to a bigger nature refuge nearby. The result won't be enough to reestablish bygone migratory patterns or room for big predators. Those elements of the heartland will have to stay confined to dreams a while longer. But, she observes, lifting her arms and circling to point to the resurgent grassland on all sides, it is a start. Even the smallest shard of prairie still seems to have the power to stretch our thoughts toward the farthest horizon.

P*rairie dogs sniff and nuzzle each other on their ancient terrain,
the South Dakota prairie. Strips of green prairie punctuate the
eroded peaks and gullies of the Badlands, a rich source of fossils
of animals here long-extinct, including rhinoceroses and camels.*

*Following pages: Racing pronghorns may be the truest form of
prairie life. This unique species is the remnant of certain horned
mammals that lived in North America 20 million years ago.*

*H*igh along the Continental Divide in Montana, a buck mule deer

makes his summertime home.

*E*lusive and independent, the mountain lion, or cougar, roams isolated, wild country hunting prey such as mule deer. Ridges and forests in the canyon of the Gallatin River are prime cougar country.

In Wyoming's Wind River Range of the Rocky Mountains, Pingora Peak

reaches toward the sky.

In a misty, steamy Yellowstone National Park, hot springs and geysers—Old Faithful at left—and elk and bison have kept each other company for millennia.

Following pages: Castle Geyser, perhaps Yellowstone's oldest, periodically bubbles and splashes, then shoots jets of steam skyward for as much as an hour. The park's thermal features remain from an era of volcanism some 600,000 years ago.

*T*he grasses of Kansas's Flint Hills shelter a bullsnake—a skillful rodent

predator that can hiss, grunt, and snort.

Land of Pronghorn and Bison

*T*he eroded sandstone pinnacle of Chimney Rock (opposite) rises above a Nebraska sea of grass. Kansas's Monument Rocks, witness to the age of dinosaurs, are remnants of shale and chalk beds of the sea that once covered much of today's grasslands.

Following pages: A bison herd thunders out of the prairie past.

FIRELIGHT BURNISHES BURIAL FIGURES FROM ETOWAH, AN ANCIENT CEREMONIAL CENTER IN GEORGIA.

Land of Deer and Turtle

*T*his is part of the balance of things: Each animal is allotted a span of existence that cannot be changed by sudden, unexpected death. If a hunter kills a deer, he should enjoy the meat in good conscience, for the blood drops will later gather and resurrect the creature so that it may go on to finish out its true life. But, as every Cherokee also learned, the hunter must offer certain words to thank the slain deer for its sacrifice and ask its pardon. The killing becomes known to the chief of the deer. Called Awi Usdi, Little Deer, he is scarcely larger than a fawn and perfectly white, like the flowers of the dogwood tree. Most of the time, he is invisible. Little Deer will arrive and ask the blood drops whether the hunter acted honorably. If the answer is no, Little Deer will follow the blood trail to the hunter's house. There, he will enter the man's body to afflict him with aches and pains that will stay with him through the rest of his days.

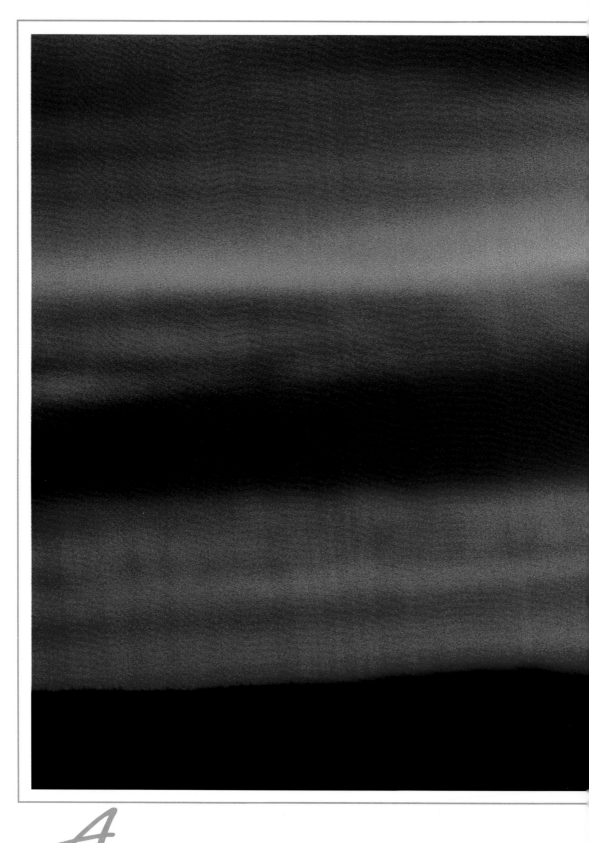

An autumn sunrise in Virginia greets a white-tailed deer at its

morning foraging. It will feed again in the evening.

This, too, is part of the balance of things. Otherwise, humans might soon forget to respect the lives of the animal tribes that share the land and waters.

Ever since the Appalachian Range formed some 300 million years ago, the East, the land of deer and turtle, has been relatively peaceful geologically. It escaped the later mountain-building epochs that wrinkled up the West and dried out the Great Basin and Great Plains. During the Ice Age, the glaciers never got their icy fingers much beyond New England, not even in the heights of the Appalachians. The present climate is generally moderate, with the highest rainfall outside the Pacific Northwest and parts of Alaska's southern coast. As a rule, the more stable and well-watered an environment is, the more generous the array of life forms that flourish in it. Before the East became the most heavily settled part of the United States, the region supported perhaps the greatest number and variety of species of any part of the country. It still does.

The East offers a wide range of habitats to begin with. As the northern coniferous forests of Canada's Maritime Provinces extend into New England, they are joined by a variety of deciduous trees, creating mixed conifer-hardwood forests. Farther south, those forests become confined to high elevations, while more and more types of broad-leaved trees that have endured from earlier geologic eras appear down below. Finally, in much of Florida and other sections of the Gulf Coast, the southern deciduous forests yield to a true subtropical environment with characteristics of the West Indies, and the East becomes the land of deer, turtle, mangrove cuckoo, alligator, and even crocodile.

Like the crocodile, many of the East's largest and most majestic creatures dwindled or disappeared altogether during the white people's era. Yet there are more kinds of salamanders, from one-inch pygmy salamanders to 29-inch hellbenders, peering from watery nooks in the southern Appalachians than big animals muscling across the vast West. And while you could cover much of the Rockies without finding close to 80 species of trees, a single grove in the Great Smoky Mountains may reveal that many as dawn brightens a hollow cupped among the hills.

Look: The spring leaves of tulip trees are interlaced with those of buckeye, basswood, magnolia, black cherry, and maples. The canopy arches far overhead. Some of the trunks supporting it are massive enough to hide a four-person tent. This hardwood stand is virgin. Primal. Ancient. The trunks were wide before the first Spanish expedition reached the area more than four centuries ago.

Spent blossoms from a Carolina silverbell tree drift down through the columned shadows and settle next to dwarf iris, showy orchis, and the hoofs of grazing white-tailed deer. Wild turkeys appear at the woodland's edge, feathers dappled the coppery color of young bark. The air is still laden with moisture exhaled by the forested slopes through the night, and the first sunlight comes soft and easy, clinging to the outline of each form like dew on spider silk. You would think the world was still just taking shape for the first time.

Beaver's grandchild, the water beetle, was the one who dived down under the waves covering the world and brought up the ball of mud that grew to become the earth. After a while, the other animals, who all lived in the sky in those days, sent turkey vulture down to see if the ground was dry yet. It was not. Turkey vulture grew so tired from searching that his wings began to strike the mud. As he was no ordinary bird but the huge ancestor of all his kind, each downward stroke sculpted a valley, and each uplift raised mountains and ridges. This is how the Smoky Mountains came to be, according to the *Yunwiya*—the Real People, the Cherokee—who call this part of the southern Appalachians their home.

The ruggedness of the countryside explains why much of it looks more or less as it did during Indian times. Like another great block of untamed land in the East—the Adirondack Mountains of upper New York, where 2.7 million acres are now protected within a state forest preserve—the Smokies resisted development long enough to become cherished for their wildness. In 1934, 520,000 acres were set aside as Great Smoky Mountains National Park. They are surrounded by more than 1.5 million acres of federal land in the form of three national forests. The combination is large enough that it may one day anchor the return of a major predator—*Canis rufus*, the red wolf, a native of the Southeast closely related to the larger

Eastern Woodlands

and more widely distributed gray wolf, *Canis lupus*. That day may not be far off. A few red wolves have already been released in the park to join the otters and peregrine falcons recently restored to the ecosystem. Recalling the Cherokee view, you could say these animals have been resurrected so that they may go on to fulfill their true span of existence.

Another carnivore walks around a pond in the valley bottom, hunting for a meal. Science classifies it among the carnivores, anyway. In practice, the animal is more an eater of roots, nuts, and insects. It is a black bear, and right now it is stalking lily bulbs. Pausing to dig, the bear notices a small creature coming from the water. It is round and low to the ground with a strange, slow gait. The bear pins it with a paw, feels a bone-hard resistance, flips the animal over, and notices that its limbs have completely disappeared.

The animal's armor is olive and yellow with swirls of red, the shell of the common painted turtle. The bear takes a tentative bite, leaving scratches between the shell's seams, rolls the turtle over a few times, and finally returns to digging. Half an hour later, the turtle has resumed its slow march, and the bear is on its way up a steep hillside. Sounds of rushing water muffle the bear's footsteps as it follows its nose past sprays of foamflowers to a rotting beech log with tasty mushrooms bulging from its surface and mouthfuls of ants to be licked up underneath. Nearby, a gray fox is putting its surprising tree-climbing skills to use in a witch hazel tree. Gripping with long, lightly furred toes, it continues on a stout limb just far enough to snatch three young hermit thrushes from a nest.

By late afternoon, the bear has passed hemlock stands on shady slopes, pine-oak stands with scarlet tanagers in the branches on dry slopes, and northern hardwood stands as it went higher yet. Topping the mountainside at last, the bear finds itself among dark spruce and fir, as if it had somehow wandered all the way to Canada. Scattered along the ridgeline are knolls with still different vegetation. Some, called heath balds, hold thickets of flaming azaleas, catawba rhododendron, and mountain laurel. Others are accurately described as grassy balds, though these low-growing meadows have their share of wildflowers, such as small forget-me-nots and and sun-loving daisies, adding to the Smokies' total of about 1,500 flowering plants.

As a rule, the sequence of habitats found from a mountain's base to its top follows the increase in rainfall and decrease in average temperatures as the altitude rises. But the existence of the balds is puzzling, for without periodic cutting or burning, they quickly become overgrown by forest. Some think lightning fires originally created the balds. Others believe the cause was grazing and trampling by heavy, hoofed animals that gathered in the high, breezy spots to escape summer's heat and insect hordes. Settlers turned out livestock to forage through these forests in decades past. Before that, the grazers would have been whitetails, elk—known among the Cherokees as the "great deer" and present in the Smokies until the 1840s—and bison. Not many people today realize that bison were so widespread that colonists hunted them along the Potomac River by what is now Washington, D.C. But then neither do many think of caribou as residents of New England during frontier times.

Upon reaching a heath bald, the bear's main concern is finding a good place to rest. It pushes into a wind-stunted clump of serviceberry, plonks down onto its rump to scratch at a tick, then rests its head upon one paw. Soon, the bear is still except for its nose, which twists now and then to catch drifting scents while a black-throated green warbler picks caterpillars from the stems and a turkey vulture drifts by, searching the ridgeline for carrion. Where its legendary ancestor fashioned the country-side with beating wings, this bird rides the afternoon thermals effort-lessly out over the procession of mountains and valleys, never flapping once before it disappears into the blue-green haze.

*F*ar to the south, a deer and a turtle greet an afternoon turned steamy. The whitetail stands on a riverbank among buttonwoods with butterfly orchids growing from their trunks and buck-thorns whose branches hold Spanish moss, ball moss, and twisted air plants—three epiphytes from the tropical bromeliad family. The turtle outweighs a black bear, can bite just as hard, and, like most fully grown alligator snapping turtles, carries gardens of algae on its back.

This is the Gulf Coast of Florida, where the biological wealth of the land joins that of the sea. The river empties into an estuary sheltered from the ocean waves by long, sandy spits and barrier islands. Here the

turtle could be a loggerhead or green sea turtle come to lay eggs high on
the beaches. Or a gopher tortoise, digging into the soil on one of the little
islands in the estuary. Its burrow, as many as 30 feet long and 12 feet
deep, will have several exit passages and turning bays in each. Like
prairie dogs in the Great Plains, gopher tortoises are a keystone species
whose tunneling activity creates habitats for many other animals: leop-
ard frogs, indigo snakes, rattlesnakes, black racers, five-lined skinks, and
Florida mice, to name a few. And opossums. When cornered, this marsu-
pial arches its back, bares its teeth, shrieks, and emits a foul-smelling
odor. Only as a last resort does it "play possum," falling onto its side
with its tongue hanging out and its heartbeat and respiration slowed to
barely detectable levels.

Most of the estuary islands are low-lying mangrove tangles. However, the one where the tortoise is at work has a hill nearly 30 feet high
near the center. From the reptile's fresh excavations, the rise appears to
consist almost entirely of mouldering fish bones and mollusk shells; those
of oysters, scallops, fighting conchs, and lightning whelks are readily rec-
ognizable. Jumbled in with them are shark teeth, segments of sea turtle
and tortoise shells, and the bones of rabbits, waterfowl, deer, raccoons,
and Caribbean monk seals. The mixture hints of a smorgasbord, and
pottery shards confirm it. The bulk of the island is anthropogenic—
human-made. Its inhabitants worked and played and prayed upon an
ever growing pile of leftovers they created from their feasting.

They were Calusa Indians. From at least 500 B.C. until shortly after
the time of European contact, they controlled a major portion of southern Florida and the Everglades, collected tribute from neighboring tribes,
and were part of a trade network that extended to the Great Lakes and
the Dakotas. In some ways, Calusa society resembled that of contempo-
rary tribes in Central America such as the Maya. At the apex was a chief,
revered as a godlike figure able to control the movements of the sun and
stars. He ruled a hierarchy of nobles, priests, and laborer castes, along
with a standing army of warriors.

For a while, the Calusa capital may have been a shell mound isle
in Estero Bay not far from the mouth of the Caloosahatchee River and the
present-day town of Fort Myers. As in other Calusa dwelling places along
the coast, the island is dissected by a system of canals leading to artificial
lagoons, called water courts, near the interior. The central mounds probably
served as ceremonial sites as well as living areas for the high-ranking classes.

Land of Deer and Turtle

Tribes throughout the East cultivated corn, beans, and squash. Many in the Southeast grew rice and tobacco as well. While the Calusa grew some squash in garden plots, virtually everything else they consumed came from fishing, hunting, and gathering. Few other native cultures maintained such a complex level of organization without a substantial agricultural base. The Calusa base lay in the solar-powered, tide-irrigated, river delta-fertilized, subtropical mangrove estuaries, which naturally produce as much food per acre as any modern farm.

ut in the shallow waters of Estero Bay, a bar of sand and silt and oysters thickens until it begins to be exposed at low tide. On the bay's inner edge, a red mangrove produces seeds. They sprout and grow several inches on the parent tree before dropping off to float away wherever the whims of wind and tide take them. One catches on the bar and begins to grow again. In time, the bulk of the plant becomes suspended above the water on a unique, stiltlike arrangement of prop roots, whose membranes have the ability to screen out salt. The roots are quickly colonized by the oysters along with mussels, barnacles, and other marine filter-feeders, and the newborn mangrove root community starts to trap a fair amount of sediments within its webwork.

As the silt piles up, black mangroves are able to establish themselves on it. More tolerant of salt than red mangroves, black mangroves have glands at the base of their leaves that excrete the compound and rootlets that stick up from the dense muck as hundreds of small, tubular snorkels—pneumatophores that improve the plants' exchange of oxygen and carbon dioxide. Leaf and twig litter builds beneath the mangroves until the ground rises above the high tide mark. White mangroves then take their turn at gaining a roothold together with buttonwood, saltwort, spider lilies, and sea purslane.

More snails and land crabs overrun the new habitat as it appears, adding their skeletons to the accumulating debris. Bird rookeries are dropping guano into the mix. Storms wash in heaps of new detritus every so often. Fiddler crabs aerate it with their burrows. Foxes, raccoons, gulls, and other hunter-gatherers create miniature versions of the Calusa middens at favorite feeding spots, building more land. Eventually, it is thick enough to be invaded by plants from patches of slightly elevated terrain, called hammocks, on the mainland.

A Calusa poling through the mangrove archipelago in a dugout canoe would probably check out any unfamiliar islands to discover what plants and animals had moved in. These Indians and their culture, however, are no more; we cannot ask them what they would do. You will have to take their place and decide what to look for. It is a leap of perspective, but from the seat of a canoe or kayak on a quiet, sunburnt afternoon, it does not seem too far.

Wading in the water and balanced on overhanging branches like tropical blossoms are tricolored herons, snowy egrets, roseate spoonbills, and white ibis, ancient tribes of birds with deep, old, raw-sounding calls. A pied-billed grebe grows alert at your approach. Instead of diving, it simply squeezes the air out from between its feathers and sinks silently out of sight. Part of another old tribe, it consumes some of its own plumage along with meals. The primitive gizzard is not very efficient at crushing the likes of sharp fish bones, and scientists think the feathers may help pad such material as it passes on into the gut.

The water is silken. Mirror images of cloud patterns float across the surface. Your thoughts begin to spread out like ripples. You find yourself contemplating the Calusa concept of souls. You have three of them: one that exists in your reflection in the water, a second in the shadow you cast, and the third shining in the pupil of your eye. When your body dies, one soul will stay with the remains. Another dissipates into the universe at large. The third will enter the body of a smaller creature. When that animal dies, the soul moves into a still smaller life form, and so on down the line of beings, the spiritual essence getting passed along like nutrients in a food chain, until it becomes so tiny that it vanishes from notice.

Suddenly, an osprey drops and splashes right next to the boat. It emerges from the spray with a mullet flapping in its talons. There must be a school of these fish passing close by, because brown pelicans are soon diving on all sides. A bottlenose porpoise circles as if herding the school, then dashes through the arc's center. Given its intelligence, curiosity, and zest for play, perhaps this inshore catcher of fish is one of the first beings the soul enters into.

Later, another large back breaks the surface—a gray, finless, slow-moving back. Paddling in that direction, you overtake a manatee female with a calf at her side. They are grazing turtle grass and widgeon grass. Though not true grasses, sea grasses are true flowering plants. They form extensive underwater pastures that, together with the mangrove forests, are largely responsible for the productivity of estuaries and their critical role in the life cycles of an estimated 70 percent of the oceans' fish.

Behind a scattering of watery islets, a more substantial island appears, and you pull in beneath the shade of its red mangrove fringe to look for a way to the interior. Each prop root is encrusted with enough oysters for a meal. The web of stalks and sharp-edged shells makes for tough walking, though, so you paddle on around the edge in hopes of finding a better route. It appears in the form of an old storm strand raised above the waterline. The shells of horseshoe crabs brought in by tides line the top and lead through black mangroves toward still higher ground and a bounty of vegetation.

There are cabbage palm with its succulent heart; coontie, whose starchy roots the Calusa pounded into flour; papaya; sea grape; pigeon plum; saffron plum; wild lime; wild caper; and wild olive. You could eat your way from the oyster beds to the treetops—while collecting Jamaica dogwood bark or coin vine to make fish poison, and Cherokee bean seeds to grind into a deadly paste to tip hunting arrows. You are brought to a halt when punctured yourself by a cat's-claw bush studded with thorns.

Resin from the tall gumbo-limbo tree will salve the wound as well as seal leaks in your boat and varnish your paddle. To sew the tear in your shirt, you could use a spine from the base of a needle palm frond or the spine from a stingray's tail.

Or, as the Calusa did, you could weave palm fibers together to make ropes for fishnets, to which you would tie wooden floats and sinkers of clam shells. The natural realm right at hand provides whatever is necessary to those who know how to look.

Land of Deer and Turtle

At present, however, the oysters of Estero Bay are too full of human-made toxins to eat. The sea grasses along Florida's coast and beyond have been drastically reduced by pollution, siltation, and dredging. The blades of countless boat propellers have also torn the pastures apart. Perhaps only 2,000 manatees remain, and you will rarely find one among them that does not have propeller scars along its back. The Florida panther is close to extinction. The snail kite of the Everglades is in serious trouble, as are the Pomacea snails it depends upon. But then the Everglades itself is struggling to survive water diversions and injections of chemicals by agricultural development upstream.

On the other hand, the brown pelican and bald eagle of the Southeast have struggled back from earlier losses with our help. The alligator population is thriving after having been nearly hunted out. Coyotes are expanding their range into the East. But development still fragments pristine wildlands, as human population increase compromises more and more open land.

Thus, the East embodies patterns of loss and hope found across the landscape to the rocky shores of the Pacific. It isn't just species that are imperiled these days. Whole ecosystems are threatened or endangered—unraveling. That tells us we are reaching or surpassing the limits of sustainable growth, because what ultimately sustains wildlife and people is the same: clean air, good water, fertile soil, and a strong, vital community fabric. Yet there is an unprecedented level of conservation activity as well. And that tells us the public is increasingly aware of the connections between our future and that of the rest of the living world. It also tells us how much people just plain want wild places and creatures around.

Our wildlife heritage consists of plants, animals, all the processes that link them, and all the miraculous tales told about nature by Indian cultures and modern science alike. As a society, we have drawn heavily upon the biological diversity of this continent for everything from industry to inspiration. Now there are so many of us that we have begun to overwhelm the source. It is time to give something back. If we can't learn how to do that, America could become a land where we know certain fierce beauties and intricately woven strengths only as things of the past. But if we can learn to share what has always been common ground, America will stand as the land of raven and bear and hawk and bison and turtle. And people. And the kind of freedom that can be found only where wildness endures.

WEARING ITS FEATHERY BREEDING PLUMAGE, A GULF COAST GREAT EGRET BUILDS ITS NEST.

*R*efuges in the beneficently watered land of a young
white-tailed deer and a Florida red-bellied turtle harbor a
multitude of animals and plants at all stages in life's cycle.

*Following pages: Under a summer storm, cabbage palmettos
stand along the seashore on a Georgia barrier island.*

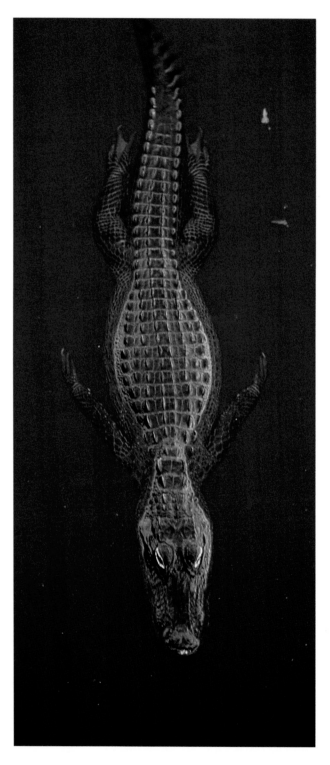
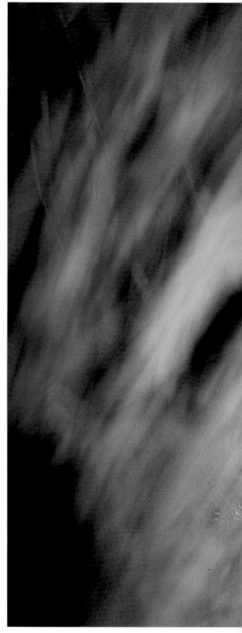

*K*in to dinosaurs, once endangered alligators today thrive in
the Florida Everglades, Georgia's Okefenokee, and other southern
swamplands. Almost 200 million years ago, their ancestors shared
these regions with apatosaurs and other long-gone creatures.

*L*ike the great egret perched amid a stand of bald cypress
(above), the little blue heron (below) and the great blue heron
regally stalk marshes, swamps, ponds, and shores.

Following pages: Against a westering sun, ibis fly homeward to
their rookery on an island sanctuary off the Florida coast.

A black bear cub clutches a tree trunk in the Great Smoky Mountains, while mosses, lichens, ferns, and shrubs make a colorful understory in a West Virginia forest. Much of the East was once home for woolly mammoths, mastodons, and other large mammals.

*W*inter chill envelopes an American white pelican. The species breeds as far north as Canada and winters from Florida westward to Mexico. In fall and winter vagrants range far and wide.

Land of Deer and Turtle

*J*ewel-like, a drop of water tips a sumac leaf as a colorful autumn carpet spreads beneath old oak trees. Oak and sumac are among gifts of the bountiful earth that Indians used for thousands of years to obtain food, medicines, and other needs.

n a fog-shrouded New Hampshire lake, a bull moose wades out,

perhaps to dip underwater for one of its favorite summer foods—water lilies.

*F*rom ferns, lichen encrusting rock,
and beautiful but deadly golden fly
amanita to spruce trees and a scarlet
autumn spread of huckleberry, Maine
mountainsides display every stage
in the millennia of evolution that
culminated in flowering plants.

Following pages: At the edge of the
continent, a new day breaks and the
old ocean endlessly ebbs and flows.

ROSY SUNRISE BATHES ALASKA'S MOUNT MCKINLEY.

Index

Library of Congress ⌖ data

Chadwick, Douglas H.

Enduring America / by Douglas H. Chadwick.
  p.   cm.
Includes index.
ISBN 0-7922-2733-6
1. North America—Pictorial works. 2. Natural history—North America—Pictorial works.
I. Title
E39.5.C43   1995
970—dc20   94-49542
                                                                  ⌖

Composition for this book by the National Geographic Society Book Division with the assistance of the Typographic section of National Geographic Production Services, Pre-Press Division. Printed and bound by R. R. Donnelley & Sons, Willard, Ohio. Color separations by Digital Color Image, Cherry Hill, N. J.; Graphic Art Service, Inc., Nashville, Tenn.; Lanman Progressive Co., Washington, D.C.; Penn Colour Graphics, Inc., Huntingdon Valley, Pa.; and Phototype Color Graphics, Pennsauken, N.J. Dust jacket printed by Miken Systems, Inc., Cheektowaga, N.Y.

DAVID MUENCH

*M*onument Valley lies on the
Utah-Arizona border.

Acknowledgments

The Book Division wishes to acknowledge the
assistance of all who have helped make possible
the publication of this volume. We are especially
grateful for the vision of Jim Brandenburg, whose
photographs of wildlife and pristine landscapes
inspired **Enduring America.**

In addition we would like to thank Robert Gibson,
University of California; Ken Imamura and Ken Whit-
ten, Alaska Department of Fish and Game; Kristie
Seaman Anders, Sanibel-Captiva Conservation Foun-
dation; Corbett McP. Torrence, Florida Museum of
Natural History; and Bruce Wing, Auke Bay Labora-
tory of the National Marine Fisheries Service.

The National Geographic Society Cartographic
Division prepared the map base for **Enduring
America.** The map relief is by Tibor G. Tóth.

Illustrations Credits

COVER: David Muench

FRONT MATTER: 1 Pat O'Hara; 2-3 Raymond Gehman; 4-5
Charles Mauzy/Tony Stone Images; 6-7 Len Rue, Jr./DRK Photo.

LAND OF WOLF AND RAVEN: 10 Art Wolfe/Tony Stone
Images; 12-13 Michio Hoshino/Minden Pictures; 23 Pat
O'Hara; 24-27 (all) Michio Hoshino/Minden Pictures; 28-31
(all) Art Wolfe; 32 Jim Brandenburg/Minden Pictures; 32-33
Art Wolfe; 34 Jeff Gnass; 34-35, 36-37 Michio Hoshino/Min-
den Pictures; 38 Jeff Gnass; 39 Joel Bennett/Tony Stone
Images; 40 Jim Brandenburg; 40-41 Jim Brandenburg/Minden
Pictures; 42-43 Jim Brandenburg.

LAND OF SALMON AND BEAR: 44 Carr Clifton/Tony Stone
Images; 46-47 Michio Hoshino/Minden Pictures; 58 Art Wolfe;
58-59 Ron Sanford/Tony Stone Images; 60-61 Art Wolfe; 62-
63 Art Wolfe/Tony Stone Images; 64 Pat O'Hara; 64-65 Carr
Clifton/Tony Stone Images; 66-67, 67 (upper) Art Wolfe; 67
(lower) Charles Mauzy/Tony Stone Images; 68-69 Art
Wolfe/Tony Stone Images; 70 (upper) Harald Sund; 70
(lower) Art Wolfe; 70-71 Pat O'Hara; 72 Jim
Brandenburg/Minden Pictures; 72-73 Marc Muench; 74 Har-
ald Sund; 74-75 Phil Schermeister; 76-77 Jim
Brandenburg/Minden Pictures; 78-79 (both) Frans
Lanting/Minden Pictures; 80-81 (both) Pat O'Hara; 82-83
David Muench.

LAND OF COYOTE AND HAWK: 84 Jeff Gnass; 86-87 Jim
Brandenburg/Minden Pictures; 97 David Hiser/Photographers
Aspen; 98 (upper) Pat O'Hara; 98 (lower) Chris Noble/Tony
Stone Images; 99 Pat O'Hara/Tony Stone Images; 100-101
Greg Probst/Tony Stone Images; 102 Jim Brandenburg/Min-
den Pictures; 102-103 Pat O'Hara; 103, 104-105 Jim Bran-
denburg/Minden Pictures; 106 David Hiser/Photographers
Aspen; 106-107 Harald Sund; 107, 108-109 David Muench;
110-111 David Ball/Tony Stone Images; 111 Carr Clifton/
Tony Stone Images; 112-113 Jim Brandenburg/Minden Pic-
tures; 113 (left) Stephen J. Krasemann/DRK Photo; 113
(right) R. Van Nostrand/Tony Stone Images; 114 David
Muench; 114-115 Tom Till; 116-117 Jim Brandenburg/Min-
den Pictures; 118-119 David Muench; 119 Carr Clifton/Tony
Stone Images; 120 David Muench; 121 Phil Schermeister/Pho-
tographers Aspen; 122-123 David Hiser/Photographers
Aspen; 124-125 (both) Art Wolfe; 126-127 Marc Muench/
Tony Stone Images.

LAND OF PRONGHORN AND BISON: 128 Chris
Johns/Tony Stone Images; 130-131, 142 Jim
Brandenburg/Minden Pictures; 143 Tom Till; 144-145 Jim
Brandenburg/Minden Pictures; 146-147, 148 Art Wolfe; 148-
149 Marc Muench; 150-153 (all) Raymond Gehman; 154-155
Pat O'Hara; 156-157 Phil Schermeister; 158-159 (both) Jeff
Gnass; 160-161 Jim Brandenburg/Minden Pictures.

LAND OF DEER AND TURTLE: 162 Lynn Johnson; 164-
165, 175 Raymond Gehman; 176-177 Carr Clifton/Tony
Stone Images; 177 (both), 178-179 Raymond Gehman; 180-
182 (all) Jim Brandenburg/Minden Pictures; 183 (upper) Art
Wolfe; 183 (lower), 184-186 Raymond Gehman; 187 David
Muench; 188-189 Jim Brandenburg; 190 Pat O'Hara; 191
Carr Clifton/Tony Stone Images; 192-193 Phil
Schermeister/Photographers Aspen; 194, 195 (upper) Carr
Clifton/Tony Stone Images; 195 (lower) Phil Schermeister;
196-197 David Muench.